HONEST
prayer

A STUDY OF THE PRAYERS OF JOB, RUTH, HANNAH, AND DAVID

Honest Prayer:

© 2022 by Sally Lombardo

All rights reserved.

Published in Houston, Texas by Bible Study Media, Inc.

Cover and Interior design by Tommy Owen Design, LLC.

ISBN # 978-1-942243-60-1
Library of Congress Control Number: 202291757

No part of this publication may be reproduced, stored in retrieval system, or transmitted in any form or by any means electronic, mechanical, photocopy, recording, or otherwise except for brief quotations in printed reviews, without the prior written permission of the publisher. www.biblestudymedia.com.

Unless otherwise indicated, all Scripture quotations are from the ESV® Bible (The Holy Bible, English Standard Version®), copyright © 2001 by Crossway, a publishing ministry of Good News Publishers. Used by permission. All rights reserved.

Printed in the United States of America

TABLE OF
contents

INTRODUCTION

Welcome	6
Introduction	8

DAILY
devotionals

Week 1	10
Week 2	26
Week 3	42
Week 4	58
Week 5	72
Week 6	88
Week 7	104
Week 8	120

STUDY
guide

Week 1	140
Week 2	144
Week 3	148
Week 4	152
Week 5	156
Week 6	160
Week 7	164
Week 8	168

APPENDICES

Frequently Asked Questions	176
Circles of Life	178
Small Group Covenant	179
Small Group Calendar	180
Prayer & Praise Journal	182
Small Group Roster	183
Small Group Leader Help	184
Leading for the First Time	185
Leadership Training 101	186

welcome

Yesterday, I sat with a friend at our favorite place, The Path of Tea. We talked about our time as hospital chaplains, and how chaplaincy is really about connecting with people we don't know at first but who we often come to know in a close way. We talked about the beautiful effects of prayer—how it calms us, invites hope into the day, and builds a bridge between our hearts and the heart of God. When you listen and pray with a patient in the hospital, no matter how awkward or brief the prayer, it becomes an intimate, life-giving journey. Prayer is just like that.

Later that day, I reflected on how prayer with God does the same thing. We begin our prayers in stumbling words, yet we become more comfortable as moments pass and words flow. We discover a presence is listening on the other side, and we are comforted. No matter how we tend to pray, most of us gain a sense of calm and renewed hope, and we feel strangely changed. This is part of God's intention and may be why he created prayer—to build a relationship with him.

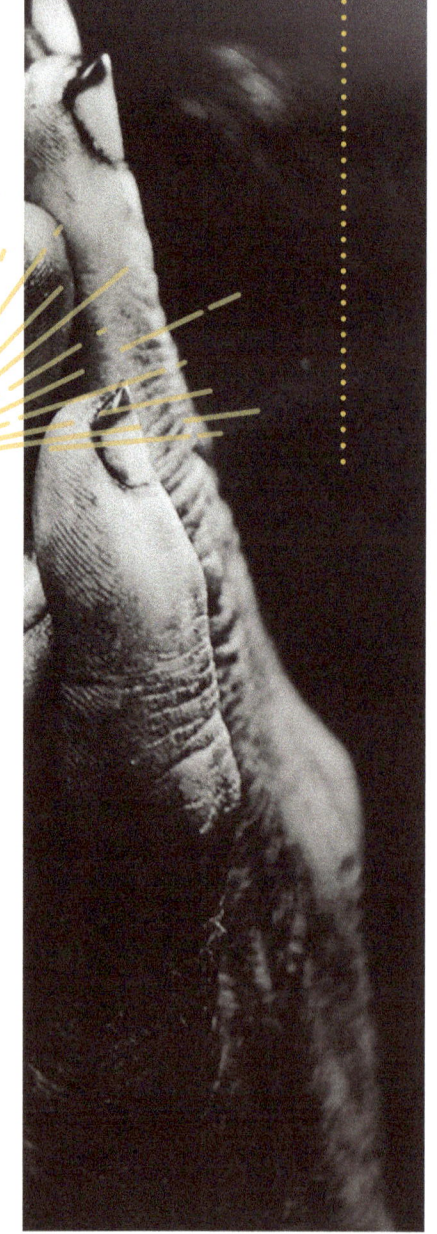

In his spiritual guidebook *Sacred Pathways,* author Gary Thomas describes the various ways people connect with God based on their spiritual temperaments. Some people are naturalists and find that walking and praying in nature is calming; some are sensates and find inspiration inside sanctuaries of stained glass; some are helpers and find God in caring for and praying with others. God has made himself apparent in the world, and we have the freedom to look for him in the ways that draw us closer. Throughout centuries, people have prayed in corporate worship, in private prayer, or in spontaneuos cries of the heart. In all its unique forms and places of expression, prayer helps us drink in God's presence, quiet our hearts, and find that while we pray, God is listening and waiting to respond.

Someone once asked Mother Teresa an interesting question about prayer: "What do you say to God when you pray?"

"I don't say anything. I just listen," she replied.

The questioner persisted: "Well then, what does God say back to you?"

"He doesn't say anything. He just listens."

As we journey into honest prayer, we will find God is listening to us, too.

Sally Lombardo
<><

introduction

Prayer prompts many questions in my life. What is a sacred prayer? How do I ask God for things that may not be part of God's will for my life? Is prayer worth my emotional effort? Does prayer change things? I struggle to be honest with my thoughts, needs, and hopes; and I wrestle with the idea that prayer should "sound good." But when I come authentically to God, I sense his presence. Honest prayer, formed from my real needs and innermost feelings, is a way to approach God with an open heart. My willingness to pray reflects my trust in God's love and promises. Persevering in prayer deepens my faith. Honest prayer opens my heart to hear wisdom and guidance from God, and my prayers become less about asking for requests and more about giving of myself.

We can't always understand life's events, but God has a bigger vision—a "super plan" for our lives when we look to him: "You will seek me and find me, when you seek me with all your heart" (Jeremiah 29:13). We can try to make sense of random events, but we should also pray for the grace, strength, and wisdom to let ourselves be used in the larger vision of God, the places where he is at work. When we are authentic, we can find peace and joy with God and recognize when he responds in unexpected moments.

Christians pray to worship and adore God, thank God for blessings, and seek his help. Often God answers with comfort, reassurance, or provision. This study will examine the heartfelt prayers of Job, Ruth, Hannah, and David, as each person prays with expectant hope that God will hear. The Lord responds abundantly. In each story, he changes attitudes, destinies, and plans, but not in the ways they expect. Job, Ruth, Hannah, and David each seek an advocate, a redeemer, a mediator, and a friend. We will explore how this looks in each story. Job suffers significant loss but finds awe and reverence for God that passes understanding. Ruth learns to trust God's providence by listening humbly. Hannah's broken heart allows God to comfort and use her for much greater things. David's last words are a succession prayer for a family line, showing how God restores and arms us with strength.

Jesus Christ is the fulfillment of each character's deepest desire. We still quote the words of Job today, and Ruth's story is still a source of hope. The Psalms are David's prayerbook, and they encourage us to trust in God and believe in the Messiah. These stories reveal ways that prayer is more than asking for our desires. Instead, prayer is a way of giving ourselves to God. Job, Ruth, Hannah, and David teach us to find wisdom in a fresh understanding of God's purpose and grace.

"You will seek me and find me, when you seek me with all your heart."

JEREMIAH 29:13

WEEK *one*

THE MYSTERY OF GOD'S SOVEREIGNTY

A righteous person acknowledges God's sovereignty.

"As for me, I would seek God, and to God would I commit my cause, who does great things and unsearchable, marvelous things without number."

JOB 5:8-9

DAY
one

WHAT IS GOD'S HEDGE OF PROTECTION?

READ JOB 1:1–13

At the beginning of this old-world story, Job was a righteous man who feared God, although he had no Scripture to read or synagogue to attend. He lived in the era of the patriarchs like Abraham and Jacob, and we wonder how he learned about Yahweh. The unknown author, who was not Job, probably had access to a tradition (oral or written) about a righteous man who endured great suffering with remarkable perseverance. Job's story must have circulated widely.

The beginning of Job is a prologue that introduces the story, setting, and tone. It is an epic tale, similar to others written in ancient times, that opens with the setting—a dry, remote area called Uz. Some scholars believe that Uz was the location of present-day Uzbekistan in central Asia, and customs in this former Soviet country reflect many of the same customs we see in Job. Job was a wealthy man with a large family, many animals, and a large spread of land; he was *"the greatest of all the people of the east"* (Job 1:3). He is described as *"a blameless and upright man, who fears God and turns away from evil"* (1: 8). Job entertains and feasts often, and he makes sure his family is purified after the feasts. Even this small fact becomes important when Job's righteousness is challenged.

We might wonder what righteousness means to God. Thankfully, it doesn't mean that God is asking us to do good works and everything right all the time. We could never do it! Instead, God provides perfect righteousness through the finished work of his Son on the cross. Through faith that Jesus died and rose again on our behalf, we are justified by faith that gives us peace (Romans 5:1). In Job, we witness a valiant struggle to understand God's sovereignty—and Job's ultimate belief that God is good and loving.

Job perseveres even when his foundation is rocked. Our own lives often mirror this wrestling, as we attempt to understand life's random events and consequences.

God defends his servant Job, saying, *"there is none like him on the earth"* (Job 1:8). Satan tries to accuse Job of hypocrisy, claiming he only fears God because of the hedge of safety placed around his life (1: 10). Satan hopes that Job will deny God and forsake his belief, but Job stands firm—and so can we. We can explore our questions and learn how to remain faithful when our plans for life go awry. The mystery is that in our prayers, God invites us to wrestle with him—and, through our struggles, to know him better.

Reflect

What might you be wrestling with in this season of life? Name two hedges of protection that you think God may have placed over you.

DAY two

THE POWER OF A DAY

READ JOB 1:13–22

On any day, we can face both joys and sorrows. Not long ago, one of my sons lost his job. He came over, looking for consolation and advice, and I mustered up words of encouragement while fighting the urge to cry. Later that same day, I was offered a job I had been praying for over the past year. I was not expecting this sudden blessing to come on the same day as my son's sudden disappointment. Thankfully, a new job for my son followed soon after. We both acknowledged these unexpected changes and the power of one day to change a life.

In the story of Job, one day changes everything, and Job's faithfulness is challenged. His seven sons and three daughters were eating and drinking in their brother's house when a great wind struck their home (Job 1:18). Did they feel a sense of foreboding or impending doom on this particular day? Probably not. Yet one frantic servant survives to tell an anguished Job that his flocks, servants, and children are all destroyed. Our first question is: Why would God allow this to happen to such a righteous man? What was God's plan through this trauma?

Job meets these events head-on by tearing his robe, shaving his head, and falling to the ground in worship and prayer. "*Naked I came...and naked shall I return. The LORD gave, and the LORD has taken away; blessed be the name of the LORD*" (Job 1:21). Job's practiced faith allows him to respond with trust in a perfect storm. In our stormy seasons, how can we trust God? We don't expect to have a rebellious child, a rift with a friend, or an argument with our spouse. But we live in a broken world. We cannot control the events of our lives; all we can control is how we cope with suffering and where we turn for help. Discipline can lay a foundation that helps us respond well, just as Job's righteous life proved to be his best defense. His obedient practices of burnt offerings, worship, and prayer laid a foundation that would serve him on even his most difficult day.

Reflect

What spiritual practices do you have that will sustain you in trouble?

DAY three

WHAT IS INTEGRITY?

READ JOB 2

We admire integrity in our world, although many people do not display it. Stories in the news describe people who do not live according to their values—and they often hide their choices and activities so others do not see who they really are. People may lie about their behavior and cover their tracks, even within the families they love. We are appalled by the degree of deception and cover-ups among people in leadership, and it leaves us wondering who to trust. Integrity is hard to find.

Job will prove himself to be a man of character and integrity. In Job 2, we meet Job's friends who come to show sympathy and offer advice, but they do not heal his deep sadness. They put dust on their heads to show that we are all set apart for destruction, but Job does not want to bury himself in ashes and admit defeat. Instead, he reminds himself of what he knows: *"Shall we receive good from God, and shall we not receive evil?"* (Job 2:10). Like Job, we may need to choose between taking advice from friends or seeking God's wisdom. Even well-meaning people may give sage advice but neglect biblical sources of wisdom—and end up feeling sorry for themselves or choosing retaliation and anger. Job makes a different choice.

Some seasons of life give us health crises, children's problems, and relationship struggles. The world says that we can avoid despair by staying busy or distracted from our pain, but Christians know a deeper truth—that our struggle can be productive. Even in times of sorrow, God provides wisdom that teaches us what avoidance cannot. *"I will instruct you and teach you in the way you should go; I will counsel you with my eye upon you"* (Psalm 32:8). We can hold fast to our integrity because God holds on to us. *"My soul clings to you; your right hand upholds me"* (Psalm 63:8).

Loyalty to our faith includes trusting the larger story; it means studying God's Word. Job remains steadfast in loyalty to God, even when his wife mocks him as he sits in despair. *"Curse God and die,"* she dismally suggests (Job 2:9). Job's struggle shows us that it's OK to lose heart and even to lament and cry while we keep walking forward. We will often wonder what God is doing in seasons where we cannot fathom his plan. Job continues to show up for his life. He believes that God is showing up, too. Job's honest words form his life of prayer.

Reflect

How do you have integrity in your prayer life? Ponder Psalm 27:14: *"Wait for the LORD; be strong, and let your heart take courage; wait for the LORD!"*

DAY

DESPAIR VS. HOPE

READ JOB 2

The movie *Gladiator* tells the story of a Roman general who bravely faces insurmountable odds. Falsely accused of a crime, Maximus is forced to become a gladiator and face terrible foes and beasts in the arena. His life appears to be over, but despite the odds against him, Maximus survives. His faith in his cause upholds him. In the end, Maximus prevails over the schemes of Commodus, the weak emperor who is full of pride—and we celebrate the gladiator's freedom and the emperor's defeat.

In chapter 3, Job summons his courage to defeat an unseen enemy. He laments his life and curses the day of his birth, and he wonders why all this has occurred (Job 3:1–12). Job faces a choice between despair and hope, between mourning his earthly losses and looking to God's sovereign comfort. We empathize with Job and wonder why God would punish him. After all, Job was a righteous man; it wasn't supposed to be this way. We wonder why doing good things, even seeking after righteousness, does not protect him.

Job ponders this same question as he questions the wisdom of his Creator. Job is caught in a web, and we see him "shaking his fist at the One who holds the world."[1] We can sympathize, but there is much more to learn. According to theologian John Goldingay, moral rules for life do not always

---

[1] Elmer B. Smick, "Job," in *The Expositor's Bible Commentary, Vol. 4,* ed. Frank E. Gaebelein (Grand Rapids, MI: Regency Reference, 1988), 889.

work to keep us free from sorrow.[2] Leading a moral life does not automatically lead to fulfillment; we need a better solution for dealing with pain.

Life is more than just being vigilant or obedient; it is choosing to believe in resurrection life and the hope that Jesus offers, even when things are hard. Because Jesus died and rose again, we can take our sorrows to God at the throne of grace (Hebrews 4:16). And when we struggle for words, the Spirit intercedes for us (Romans 8:26). Our prayers lead us to abundant fellowship with God.

The hope of God's restoration and renewal is the story of Job. "Where God's promise of life still exists, hope exists," Goldingay observes, and "Job's love for God keeps him hoping the sun will finally rise and the tide will turn."[3]

Reflect

When have you chosen between despair or hope? How did this turn out for you?

---

2   John Goldingay, *Old Testament Theology: Israel's Faith: Vol II* (Downers Grove, IL: InterVarsity Press, 2016), 618.
3   Goldingay, 618.

DAY

CAN WE TRUST OUR FRIENDS?

READ JOB 4–6

Eugene Peterson often wrote about the importance of following God in all seasons. In *A Long Obedience in the Same Direction*, Peterson uses the Psalms of Ascent to show that even in our walks with Christ, we will encounter both joy and disappointment. When we exclusively consult friends for encouragement or watch what others are doing, we lose focus on God's truth. "The great danger of Christian discipleship," he says, "is that we should have two religions: a glorious, Sunday gospel that sets us free from the world, that in the cross and resurrection of Christ makes eternity alive in us, a magnificent gospel of Genesis and Romans and Revelation; and, then, an everyday religion that we make do with during the week…the everyday religion of the *Reader's Digest* reprint, advice from a friend, an Ann Landers column, the huckstered wisdom of a talk-show celebrity."[1]

In chapter 4, Job's friend Eliphaz gives a simplistic answer that he thinks will comfort Job. He suggests that God is just, reasonable, and logical—that he rewards the righteous and punishes the wicked. Wouldn't life be easy if this eye-for-an-eye mentality were always true? Yet, given the reality of people's lives and the confusing nature of cultural trends and thoughts, Eliphaz's argument is weak, and his explanation does not help us cope with true sorrow and loss. In honesty, Eliphaz's platitude about life doesn't even work for Job.

---

1 Eugene Peterson, *A Long Obedience in the Same Direction: Discipleship in an Instant Society* (Downers Grove, IL: InterVarsity Press, 2000), 44.

However, he offers one piece of advice that proves prophetic: *"As for me, I would seek God, and to God I would commit my cause, who does things great and unsearchable, marvelous things without number"* (Job 5:8–9). This faithful trust in God is what Job will display in his prayers.

If we turn to our friends alone, we often find weak counsel. Humans have a limited understanding of God's larger plan in the world and in our lives. God asks us to look upward to him instead of comparing ourselves to others, because he alone understands our hurts and deepest needs. The challenging book of Job deals with God's divine justice, a complex subject, and we will explore this as we walk through Job's argument with God. While we cannot understand the reasons behind much of our suffering, we can trust that God sees the bigger picture and can give us hope when we pray from the heart.

Reflect

Consider times when you have looked to others for wisdom. Has their advice helped, or has it led you astray?

DAY six

LORD, SEND ME AN ARBITER

READ JOB 7–10

We live in a litigious society. There are lawyers for every aspect of life—and we have three in our family. My sons' legal skills are so specialized that I usually call a different son for each specific question. In our conflicted world, we need people to help mediate disputes. Families who suffer disagreements need arbiters and mediators to help. An arbiter works on behalf of both parties, but in the end, the arbiter has the ultimate authority to decide.

In chapters 7–10, Job is at a breaking point. In desperation, he throws up his hands and complains that his flesh has maggots. He cries out to God. "*I would choose strangling and death rather than my bones…Leave me alone, for my days are a breath*" (Job 7:15–16). Job's words make us cringe. His fears and anger seem justified, and we are unsettled by the possibility of a capricious God. We see the evidence of righteous Job, and it seems like there is no real case against him. Job appears innocent of wrongdoing, and yet Satan accuses him.

Job is innocent of Satan's accusations of blasphemy. He has not rejected God or forsaken his faith, so what is God doing here, and when will legal counsel arrive to plead his case? Today, we know arbiters as people who explain and try a case for someone who has been misunderstood. This early picture of a mediator is not much different. Job finally suggests to God, "*Why do you not pardon my transgression and take away my iniquity?*" (7:21). His question is an authentic and honest cry for help from a person who can see the truth of what has occurred. He voices a prayer that one day God will fulfill by sending the Son who died to gain our pardon.

On the one hand, Job's story is a forerunner of Jesus, a man hated and accused of evil he did not do. But Job was not perfect (13:23, 26), and when he meets God, he repents (40:4–5; 42:2). Jesus, on the other hand, was perfectly righteous. He was tempted and suffered, but he never sinned (2

Corinthians 5:21).

So Job's honest prayer invites a question: Who can settle the disagreement between God and sinful man? The only righteous Man, the only suitable Mediator, is Christ, who suffered to pay for the sins that separate us from God. "*There is no arbiter between us, who might lay his hand on us both. Let [God] take his rod away from me, and let not the dread of him terrify me,*" Job cries (9:33–34). Centuries after Job, God would remove the rod from humanity and send the awaited Man.

Reflect

When have you needed the mediation of Jesus Christ?

DAY
seven

YET THOUGH HE SLAY ME, I WILL FOLLOW

READ JOB 12–14

Flannery O'Connor wrote stories with religious themes characterizing the "action of grace in territory held by the devil."[1] In "A Good Man is Hard to Find," O'Connor describes a family who is stranded after a wreck. They hope for a rescuer to save them, but none arrives. They become frantic with the desire to be rescued. Instead, an escaped criminal comes down the road and feigns concern. Slowly, he takes everything they have, which results in disaster. The outcome doesn't make sense, as the family has done nothing wrong. The grandmother questions the felon's choice, and he replies, "Nome, I ain't a good man... Does it seem right to you, lady, that one is punished a heap, and another ain't punished at all?"[2]

This irony stumps us when we encounter unfairness. For reasons beyond Job's understanding, Satan has permission to torment him, and Job wrestles with his pain. Some people experience far beyond a fair share of trials. Righteous friends become ill, immoral people rise to fame, and sudden tragedies bring chaos and despair. How do we make sense of this, when we know that God is love? We live in a fallen world where morality and good living do not keep us safe from pain. The current global health crisis is an example, as the virus favored no one and affected everyone. Families have suffered. To-

---

1   X. J. Kennedy and Dana Gioia, "Flannery O'Connor" in *Backpack Literature: An Introduction to Fiction, Poetry, Drama, and Writing* (New York: Pearson, 2016), 419.
2   Kennedy and Giola, *Backpack LIterature,* 228.

day, we don't know how COVID will end, but we continue to work, learn, and care for those we love.

Job's suffering has taken a mental and emotional toll. When Job announces, "*Yet though he slay me, I will hope in him; yet I will argue my ways to his face. This will be my salvation*' (13:15–16), his friends are dismayed. How can this man still hope in God? Job hopes because he remembers God's goodness. We can assure ourselves of God's love by remembering times that strengthened our faith. Reflect on ways that God has strengthened you during the pandemic and notice the hedges of protection God provides. See how God has encouraged you through prayer and the support of a community of faith.

Reflect

How has God shown his faithfulness to you this year?

WEEK *two*

LISTENING

TO

THE

COUNSEL

OF

FRIENDS

Humility is found in recognizing who God is
and seeking him alone.

"Even now, behold, my witness is in heaven."

JOB 16:19

DAY eight

EARTH, COVER MY BLOOD

READ JOB 15–17

In the story of Cain and Abel, God asks Cain, "*Where is Abel your brother? … What have you done? Your voice of your brother's blood is crying to me from the ground…which has opened its mouth to receive your brother's blood*" (Genesis 4:9–11). A professor I had in seminary explained that the Hebrew translation of this verse is closer to: "Abel's blood opens now the gaping mouth of the earth." The monstrous imagery has stayed with me, reminding me how Cain's deceit provoked the earth to open its mouth like a prehistoric beast. Figuratively, this shows how God's earth must absorb man's evil deeds.

Suffering is painful and gruesome at times. Job's three counselors are well-meaning friends but cannot cover their friend with enough advice. Their explanations put the responsibility on man to do what is right; they do not cite God's mercy or the Messiah's role to cover our blood. Eliphaz claims that people must suffer, and righteous people will find peace. Yet Job is not wicked, so the equation falls apart. Job has not found peace. We face the same dilemma: No human is perfect in thought, word, or deed, and we are not immune to the consequences of sin. The book of Genesis tells the story of our original sin in the garden. Our noble efforts cannot redeem us from our tendency to run from God or our guilt. We need God's grace through redemption and rescue.

A friend of mine recently lost her father to opioid addiction. His family had tried desperately to love him, challenge him, and change him. The man himself tried many escape routes, but because of his ongoing pain and the all-too-available painkillers, he eventually lost the battle. We are helpless to save ourselves from impossible dilemmas, and we need rescue. Job wavers between hope and despair, but in the end, he finds hope in God's mercy: "*Even now, behold, my witness is in heaven, and he who testifies for me is on high.*" (Job 16:19).

Reflect

How do you find comfort in God's instruction and counsel in times of struggle?

DAY

DO YOU KNOW THAT YOUR REDEEMER LIVES?

READ JOB 19–20

The church fathers were teachers and theologians in the Patristic Era (AD 100–700) who laid the foundations of Christianity. Polycarp, bishop of Smyrna, was one of these brave men and a disciple of John. This man of faith was arrested for heresy and tortured by fire, yet he refused to renounce Christ. "God has done me no wrong," he said. "How can I blaspheme my King and my Redeemer?"[1] Legend claims that a dove flew out of Polycarp's chest at his death.

With the same fearless loyalty, Job stands up to his friends. Job admits that "*the hand of God has struck me*" (Job 19:21), but vows that he is not forsaken. Satan hoped that if God took everything from Job, Job would curse God. Instead, Job looks to God for rescue: *"For I know that my Redeemer lives, and at the last he will stand upon the earth,"* he claims (19:25). Job asks: How can I blaspheme my only hope for a redeemer? The verb *redeem* signifies compensation for a fault or shortcoming or payment to buy back something that was lost. God planted the need for redemption in the heart of the story of Israel. Levitical law dictated that "*If your brother becomes poor and sells part of his property, then his nearest redeemer shall come and redeem what his brother has sold*" (Leviticus 25:25). God's people knew they would need redemption in many ways.

We may not need someone to buy our land or rescue our family, but we do need God to redeem our shortcomings—our selfish actions, past re-

---

[1] Michael Holmes, *The Apostolic Fathers* (Downers Grove, IL: IVP), 121.

grets, or harsh words. We need loving Christian community. We are dependent on God's rescue from the penalty, or "*wages of sin*" that are death (Romans 6:23), or we will experience a life of dead-ends that do not bear eternal fruit. Only Jesus, who came to rescue and redeem fallen man, can infuse our lives with meaning and purpose for his larger will. He is the author of the "super plan" that guides us toward his kingdom, on earth and in heaven. Thanks be to God that he chose to provide a Redeemer in Christ, a divine Kinsman who bought our spiritual freedom and restored friendship with God.

Reflect

From what fears, habits, or practices do you need a rescue?

DAY

GOD PURSUES US IN OUR PAIN

READ JOB 21–22

English poet Francis Thompson composed a mystic poem entitled "The Hound of Heaven," which tells the story of a man pursued by the relentless love of Christ, who will not let him go. "I fled him down the winding stairs, and in the mist of tears…through my nights and days, and in my many fears," the poem reads.[1] "The name is so strange," says Jesuit Father John Francis O'Conor. "But when one reads the poem, this strangeness disappears. As the hound draws nearer in the chase…we see how God follows the fleeing soul by Divine grace."[2]

We, too, run from God when life seems unfair, but God chases us. We get mad, become depressed, or shut down. The prophet Elijah, having just slit the throats of the prophets of Baal at God's command, is exhausted and afraid. He runs to a broom tree where he can rest and hide, then begs God not to use him as his prophet. *"It is enough; now, O LORD, take away my life, for I am no better than my fathers"* (1 Kings 19:4). God hears Elijah and sends an angel to feed him. In his mercy, God supplies Elijah with food, shelter, and shade, encouraging him to walk on.

Job does not run from God but struggles with the question, *"Why do the wicked live…grow mighty in power…and spend their days in prosperity?"*

---

1   Francis Thompson, "The Hound of Heaven," www.houndofheaven.com/poem.
2   John Francis Xavier O'Conor. *A Study of Francis Thompson's Hound of Heaven* (New York: John Lane Company, 1912), 7.

(Job 21:7, 13). He is broken in his suffering, but ironically, it is Job's high view of God that brings about his struggle. If we don't long to know God or believe him, we don't wrestle with what God is and is not. Job is a person who believes in God's love enough to wrestle.

Just like Job, our heaven-sent questions often go unanswered. As in other wisdom writing, God's purposes here remain a mystery, but the Lord calls us to faith. During some seasons, we are called to act, love, and serve. During all times, we are called to pray (1 Thessalonians 5:17). Even when we don't understand why things happen as they do, God offers mercy and hope through his Word, through the sacraments, through our spiritual practices, and through the love of family and friends. Just as with Elijah, God supplies what we need to walk on.

Reflect

What are some hard questions you wrestle with?

DAY

DRAW US CLOSE

READ JOB 23–24

Sometimes we believe that we are being tested, just as Job did, and we don't feel like drawing close to God. We wonder how to endure the storm and hold fast to our belief in God's goodness despite the confusion. I recently met a godly woman who is part of a church staff. She made a tough decision but is now feeling abandoned by God. After she accepted a pastoral care position in her church, she experienced betrayal by a staff member and became confused that her choice did not bear fruit. "I trusted you, God," she prayed. "I thought I was obeying when I took this job." We met during a time of retreat to talk about questions and pray for the Spirit's help. We discussed the reality that God is still shaping her through the confusion and pain.

With characteristic honesty, Job agonizes in prayer and asks God why he is not there when Job needs him most! He tries to justify, explain, and act as his own advocate. As he pleads his case to find a witness who will testify, he is confused and disappointed. But no one steps up. Job waits to dialogue with God and continues to ask for God's presence. God will answer, but as readers, we don't know when. In our own lives, we will not see all things healed until the appointed time, but we can sense God's answers and feel him at work in our lives. We can look for God's guidance through godly friends, answered prayer, and time in his Word.

Job concludes that his only hope is to draw close to God, just as my friend is doing. She continues to seek God in spiritual practices, and her life now has new direction. Trials in our lives are more than just tests of valor; they are opportunities to grow closer to God. Sometimes passing the test can mean staying strong in our faith and setting up our guardrails of honest prayer. One of my guardrails is to ask God what he may be trying to teach me through trials. When storms make us feel lost, we can ask God what he might be showing us; we can plead with him to continue to draw us close.

Reflect

Where do you look when you are afraid or when God seems silent?

DAY

WHERE DO I FIND GOD?

READ JOB 26–27

We often try to find God by looking up to heaven. We imagine God that is up there watching over us and that heaven is his home. We love the idea of eternity. The writer of Ecclesiastes tells us that God *"has made everything beautiful in its time…he has put eternity into man's heart"* (3:11). This spring, I was hiking and watched a white-headed eagle swooping towards a small nest in the pines. A tiny swallow with an orange face was making sudden, darting attempts to ward the eagle off from her young. The bird was relentless, and the eagle finally flew away. I was astounded at the bird's power against its predator.

Job is watching a similar drama play out, as his friends use persuasion and rhetoric to drive home their arguments. His voice is small, but it has power because it continues to honor God. While his friends compete for airtime, Job asks them: What advice or wisdom have you offered me? *"With whose help have you uttered words, and whose breath has come out from you?"* (Job 26:4). Instead of looking for wisdom from his friends, Job looks to God. He recounts God's mighty actions and praises his strength, striking the humble pose he will maintain for the rest of the story. God is a mystery. *"But the thunder of his power who can understand?"* Job asks (26:14).

The small bird's courage inspired me. I saw God's glory in a tiny creature that remained resolved and undaunted by opposition. As I watched the birds swoop and fly, something else took place. A second, tinier bird came out to aid the first as she protected her young. With the same orange coloring as the first bird, the second bird flew around the first as if to say, "I am here!" Then she proceeded to chase the eagle along with her friend. Her effort was valiant and made me smile. The concerns that had weighed upon my heart began to vanish.

The birds' natural drama calmed and quieted my heart and reminded me that we don't struggle alone. We have brothers and sisters to come alongside us in faith, that we "*may be encouraged, being knit together in love, to reach all the riches of full assurance of understanding and the knowledge of God's mystery, which is Christ, in whom are hidden all the treasures of wisdom and knowledge*" (Colossians 2:2–3).

Reflect

What emotions do you feel when you look up to see the beauty of the heavens?

DAY Thirteen

WHERE CAN WISDOM BE FOUND?

READ JOB 28

When my four boys were young, I used to gather them around our worn kitchen table to read the Bible together, usually from the Psalms or Proverbs. I especially liked to read to my children about wisdom because I knew they would need biblical wisdom more than they needed good grades or accomplished lives. I am still hopeful that those evenings around the table have paid off. Wisdom is something you incorporate over many seasons.

Job 28 is known as the Wisdom Chapter, or a Hymn to Wisdom. Since God is referred to in the hymn as *Adonai* and not *Yahweh*, the hymn may have been a later addition to the narrative—but its words reinforce the unsearchable nature of God that defies man's ability to understand. Theologian Elmer Smick calls the chapter a poetic interlude that describes the "elusive nature of wisdom, which is only attained through true submission."[1] Job finds peace as he accepts God's true interpretation of life.

The poetic hymn is built around descriptions of the mining work common in ancient Palestine, and the author compares the search for gold to man's continual search for God. Chapter 28 suggests that wisdom is not found in a *"bird of prey"* or the *"proud beasts"* (28:7–8). It cannot be grasped on ocean or land, bought with gold, or obtained through man's achievement (28:14–15). Job's humble conclusion is that wisdom is not a place or event, and it is not based on human knowledge. It is grounded in *"the fear of the LORD, that is wisdom, and to turn away from evil is understanding"* (28:28).

---

[1] Smick, "Job," 975.

We are surprised that fear is the beginning of wisdom because we are taught to think that fear is an emotion we should overcome. But this is not what fear meant to ancient minds. Healthy fear was a mixture of dread and reverence, a respect for the presence of the Almighty. Fear could save your life. Today, society values control and feats of strength, and many people resent the idea of God's authority or submission to something greater than themselves. We know how quickly life can change and how often our control is lost. In Job's time, men feared many things about the natural world, and it was considered noble to pray for God's protection and strength in times of trial and uncertainty. We are wise to do the same.

Reflect

What one or two Bible verses help you gain strength from God's wisdom?

DAY fourteen

"LUNCH-MONEY FAITH"

READ JOB 29–30

Contemporary author Anne Lamott writes essays that describe ordinary ways to navigate the unexpected in life. Recently I read "Lunch-Money Faith," which describes a spiritual practice that challenges our definitions. Faith is more than just being a good sport about things that come, writes Lamott; faith supplies our basic needs so we can keep standing. Faith is enough to get us by. "Why are we even in the world?" Lamott asks. "We are here to learn about life, to grow up, to come to understand what is real....We are not here to pretend to be doing fine. We just need to have more lunch-money faith."[1]

In chapter 29, Job is exhausted. He has been trying to understand God's ways and the reasons behind his misfortune, and it's all too hard. He longs to return to the faith of a peaceful fellowship with God: "*O that I were as in the months of old, as in the days when God watched over me, when his lamp shone upon my head*" (29:2–3). Job is tired and even angry at God. When he tries to understand his suffering, he ends up back at square one. "*When I hoped for good, evil came, and when I waited for light, darkness came*" (30:26). His questions are those of people who suffer in ways that seem random and impossible to understand.

Job makes a final appeal to God. In our lives, this might look like finding just enough faith to supply our needs. Sometimes spending time in nature helps us know that God is real. Friends can help us heal, and family can support us through sorrow. Keeping a gratitude journal boosts our spirits and

---

1   Anne Lamott, *Dusk, Night, Dawn* (New York: Riverhead Books, 2021), 109–110.

guards our hearts. If we rely on the fact that God has given us our daily bread, we can find peace. Sometimes this daily bread is an assurance that God is there and that we can rest in him. Other times it is warm moments with family or a laugh with a friend. This kind of genuine fellowship can be just enough to buy us some lunch, to carry us over until the world looks hopeful again.

Reflect

What has God done for you this week that has been "just enough" for you?

WEEK

SEEKING

GOD

AS

A

MEDIATOR

We must watch for God and listen while we wait.

"For God speaks again and again, though people do not recognize it. He speaks in dreams, in visions of the night."

JOB 33:14–15 NLT

DAY

DOES GOD SEE ME?

READ JOB 31

    1 Kings 17–19 tells the story of Elijah, who was a bit of a curmudgeon, but also a brave soul who had a life of miracles. God commissioned Elijah to travel to a remote, dry riverbed (the Wadi Cherith) and be fed by ravens. Then he stayed with a widow, made her jar of flour last a year, and raised her teenage son from the dead. Soon after this, Elijah was commanded to shame the two hundred prophets of Baal by bringing down fire on an altar, then causing rain to fall. After such triumph, Jezebel's emissaries chased Elijah to kill him, and he hid in the desert under a broom tree. After all the miracles, he asked God if he could die because he had failed his ancestors. He knew that God saw and heard him, so his prayer was voiced in a kind of faith. God responded to Elijah by sending food, a strong wind, an earthquake, and a whisper.

    Like Elijah, Job finds himself in a desperate place. In a flurry of tears and anger, Job begs to be seen by God, and he wants much more than a whisper. He pleads, "*Oh, that I had one to hear me! Here is my signature! Let the Almighty answer me!*" (31:35). Job defends himself and tries to draw up a covenant that God will sign. He tries to bargain with God, whose silence has become unbearable. For reasons unexplained, God makes Job wait. Just as with Elijah, God allows Job to stew in silence until he is ready to listen.

    Richard Rohr comments on how we can learn to find God in silence. He describes a kind of "waiting room" where we may not want to wait. We will do anything to avoid this "terrible cloud of unknowing," says Rohr, yet only a person who has waited alone in dark moments can help others learn how to wait on God.[1] Most Christians shrink from this high calling. Maybe we are being prepared for ministry or a greater calling in life. We can continue to pray and take care of our hearts through the darkness of waiting, knowing that God will eventually speak. We can trust that he hears our cries for help.

Reflect

When have you been comfortable with silence?

---

1 Ruth Haley Barton, *Strengthening the Soul of Your Leadership* (Downers Grove, IL: IVP, 2018), 97–98.

DAY sixteen

GOD SPEAKS IN WAYS MAN MAY NOT PERCEIVE

READ JOB 32–33:18

In *The Problem of Pain*, C. S. Lewis observes that "God whispers to us in our pleasures, speaks in our conscience, but shouts in our pain. It is his megaphone to rouse a deaf world."[1] For some reason, we don't often hear God in our pleasures. But through our pain, God speaks volumes. Consider the recent pandemic we all have faced. We were unaware of the benefit of wearing masks until statistics showed their effectiveness. The virus has been like a megaphone, and the accompanying civil unrest has opened our eyes in many ways.

Trusting that God is acting in world events helps us listen to his voice. It helps us understand how these events are shouting at us to change our negligent ways. Pain opens our spiritual eyes, hones our spiritual radar, and drives us closer to God. In chapter 32, Elihu states that man's rationale and ability to achieve do not provide answers to our deepest needs; rather, it is God's Spirit, *"the breath of the Almighty, that makes him understand"* (Job 32:8).

Elihu insists that God is speaking to us, if we will only see it. "*The breath of the Almighty gives me life*" (33:4). He also demands that Job stand up and argue his case, just as God will do for him down the line. Elihu reminds Job to pray, for when "*man prays to God, and he accepts him, he sees his face with a shout of joy, and he restores to man his righteousness*" (33:26). He encourages Job to look for ways that God is speaking, and this

---

[1] C. S. Lewis, *The Problem of Pain* (London: Oxford UP, 1966), 15.

encouragement also challenges us. God gives his people support in trials and struggles by refining them. Elihu's message is not far from the apostle Paul's encouragement to the Roman church: *"We rejoice in our sufferings, knowing that our suffering produces endurance, and endurance produces character, and character produces hope"* (Romans 5:3). In his suffering, Job looks to God and finds hope that, at first, he did not see.

Reflect

During a time of suffering in your life, how did God's Word speak to you through your pain?

DAY

IS THERE AN ANGEL AT YOUR SIDE?

READ JOB 33:19–34

We have angels all wrong. Someday, we will need to apologize to them. Picture standing before Gabriel or Michael and saying, "We are sorry we painted you like small cherubs." Angels are fearsome creatures who look like men but have faces like lightning and eyes like flaming torches (Daniel 10:6). They are dispatched by God in response to prayer, supplication, and desperation. When an angel approaches a Bible hero, the recipient of its message is usually terrified and falls prostrate. Biblical angels are not cute. They may bring comfort, but they often foretell coming doom—so there is a justified reason for fear.

Throughout the Old Testament, angels were majestic messengers. Angels announced the birth of the Messiah (Matthew 1:20–25), sustained the Lord in his earthly ministry (Mark 1:13), and helped the apostles fulfill the calling of Christ in the early church (Acts 5:17–20; 12:5–11). Elihu promises that if an angel appears, that same angel may choose to beseech God on man's behalf. *"If there be for him an angel, a mediator, one of the thousand, to declare to man what is right for him, and he is merciful to him, and says, 'Deliver him from going down into the pit; I have found a ransom'"* (33:23–24). A mediator communicates between two persons, just as an angel does for people who follow God.

Hebrews 13:2 warns us that we might mistake the appearance of an angel. One Sunday after church, a smiling woman wearing a purple suit broke into the line beside me at Luby's. This kind woman helped my four little boys, who were reaching into the buffet for French fries and chocolate pies, to get their trays. She balanced their food on the trays as I frantically balanced my baby girl on my hip and my tray in my hands. After thanking her profusely as we all sat down, I looked up, and she was gone.
One of my little boys asked, "Mom, who was that?" I thought she must have

been some kind of angel at my side.
Reflect

Recall chance encounters with people who lifted your heart. Is there a time that God comforted you unexpectedly?

DAY eighteen

GOD, TEACH ME WHAT I DO NOT SEE

READ JOB 34–35

The Message Bible translates Proverbs 3:5–6 in a unique way: "*Trust God from the bottom of your heart; don't try to figure everything out on your own. Listen for God's voice in everything you do, everywhere you go; he's the one who will keep you on track.*" I like this simple explanation, especially the part about not trying to figure everything out on our own. When I'm confused, I look to stories in the Bible about people who were flawed and afraid but didn't try to figure everything out. Many things remain unexplained in our lives, but that does not mean that God is not real, that his promises are not true, or that his love is not steadfast.

Elihu, on the other hand, continues to try to make sense of the inexplicable. He is certain that God repays us for our choices, according to what our conduct deserves. Job's dilemma perplexes him because he has not shown poor conduct, made bad choices, or done evil things. Elihu describes God as something like a mean teacher who reprimands his students. If God chooses, says Elihu, men will just "*return to dust*" and cease to exist (Job 34:15). This caricature of God is not comforting and does not draw us to him. After his long and breathless testimony, Elihu finally asks God: "*Teach me what I do not see; if I have done iniquity, I will do it no more*" (34:32). His humility guides him, and Job arrives at the same conclusion.

What do we need to learn that we do not see? During his wilderness temptation, Jesus redirected Satan's accusing questions to focus on God's innate goodness. God's provision is all around us. Jesus described the Father as one who welcomes us into his love, supplies our needs, and gives us more than bread alone. We can thank God that we have his promises, commandments, and rules for life. When reality is too hard to understand, and a divine-justice mentality won't suffice, it is better "*to trust God from the bottom of your heart*" and lean not on the things we cannot see or understand (Proverbs 3:5 MSG).

Reflect

What are some things God provides that you cannot see with human eyes?

DAY

GIVE ME STRENGTH OF HEART

READ JOB 36–37

A song by Christian artist Laura Story describes finding perfect peace in God. "In your time of need," she writes, "pain that no one sees...trust Me when I say, that I will give you perfect peace."[1] I have often stopped to pray for such peace. Worries about my children's futures or regrets about my own life can disturb my sense of peace. Even in our hurried efforts, there is still a yawning emptiness that no amount of positive activity can fill. This emptiness can result from not resting in God and striving to make life work in our own ways.

Elihu tries to speak on God's behalf: "*Behold, God is mighty, and does not despise any; he is mighty in strength of understanding*" (36:5). Another translation of the same verse says, "*God is mighty in strength of heart*" (36:5 NLT). The word *heart* in ancient Hebrew encompassed everything—mind (wisdom), will (purpose), and emotions (love). God's three-channeled heart enables him to deal with us with compassion, purpose, and design.[2] We can draw near to the heart of God the Father through the help of the Spirit and the intercession of the Son.

God delivers those who suffer and "*speaks to them in their affliction*," Elihu promises (36:15 NIV). Even when we don't see a way out, God speaks to us in the midst of our affliction and emptiness—if we will listen. Even if he

---

1   "Blessings," Laura Story Music, October 29, 2013, https://www.youtube.com/watch?v=JKPeoPiK9XE.
2   Textual note, *Holman Christian Standard Bible* (Nashville, TN: Holman Bible Publishers, 2009), 865.

does not deliver us from disappointment on earth, God's compassion dictates that he must respond, and his sovereign will charts a path forward for each of us. He provides the strength we need to carry on. Ruth Haley Barton suggests that our modern epidemic of loneliness, bitterness, and despair has produced despondency, but God can fill that emptiness if we will only look to him.[3] We long for God to provide the perfect peace that only he can offer. Knowing the everlasting character of God as Father, Son, and Holy Spirit can give us the strength of heart we need.

Reflect

Describe a time when God filled you with a sense of peace and strength of heart, even when things didn't make sense.

---

[3] Ruth Haley Barton, *Strengthening the Soul of Your Leadership,* 43.

DAY twenty

DRESS FOR ACTION

READ JOB 38:1–21

After all is said between Job and his friends, God speaks with Job. We take this theophany for granted, but it is given to precious few. Job's mighty struggle has been won, and it was worth the wrestling. God questions Job face to face, just as he appeared to Moses in a burning bush and in a cloud on Sinai. For this audience, Job must "*dress for action like a man*" who is heading to a trial (Job 38:3). Yet there is no testimony here; Job never says a word in his defense. We picture Job quaking before God, mesmerized and in awe of his sovereign Creator.

Job has been profoundly changed. He has stood up to the passionate arguments of his friends and the testing of his faith. Now God teaches Job with authoritative, wise counsel. Job's humble posture represents the stance of a disciple who sits at a teacher's feet to learn. He bravely faces the mystery of God, so he can know with certainty that God is all he needs.

There is something about arrogance and pride that makes us spiritually deaf. When people vie for power—in relationships, the business world, and even in church congregations—they stop hearing from God. The human desire for control displaces humility and alienates people from each other. Jesus warned, "*Whoever exalts himself will be humbled, and whoever humbles himself will be exalted*" (Matthew 23:12). Without a teachable spirit, we are out of God's reach, unaware of our need for his hope, and unable to hear his instruction.

To hear from God, we have to stop trying to play the role of God. As Job hears more clearly, he is released from having to know and explain all things. "*Have you given orders to the morning, or…journeyed to the springs of the sea?*" God asks (Job 38:12, 16 NIV). "*Have the gates of death been revealed to you, or have you seen the gates of deep darkness?*" (38:17). If you have stood on a beach and watched a storm come in, you quickly realize your smallness. Man cannot hold back a hurricane, reverse the spread of disease, or fix a broken heart. But God can enter our lives in his direct, piercing way and offer true healing. Only when we pray honestly to God can we find the intimacy that will satisfy us. We can pray, *"Show me now your ways, that I may know you in order to find favor in your sight"* (Exodus 33:13).

Reflect

What could you change to hear from God more clearly?

DAY twenty-one

GOD'S SILENCE

READ JOB 38:2–41

A favorite book on my shelf is *Troubling Deaf Heaven*, written by a dear friend, Christian actress, and community leader. Jeannette Clift George wrote several books about God's whispers and his desire to communicate with us in unexpected ways. *Troubling Deaf Heaven* asks, "What do we do when faced with the silence of God?" We sometimes wonder if God may be deaf or why he isn't answering. The title is a quote from Shakespeare, and in her book, Jeannette poses questions like, "What do we do when everyone is getting faxes from God, and our prayers bounce back from the ceiling?"[1]

We may question God's silence and compare it to our own passive inattention to others or our choice to withdraw. But God is not like us. Scripture says that he never sleeps (Psalm 121:3–4), and he does not remove his Spirit from a believer, even when we sin (Ephesians 1:13–14). Sometimes we may keep our deepest hurt from God, and we cannot draw close to God during these times since we have built a wall. Yet even then, we remain in God's care, not because of our "unfaltering faith but because of his unfaltering grip on our lives."[2]

Job has been "troubling deaf heaven" for some time now, wondering where his advocate, mediator, and redeemer might be. In chapter 38, God answers, but not as the grand defender Job had hoped for. God doesn't explain his ways or his past silence, but Job doesn't ask him to. Think of

---

1 Jeanette Clift George, *Troubling Deaf Heaven* (Nashville: Broadman & Holman, 2005), 2.
2 George, *Troubling Deaf Heaven*, 4.

the times you may have wanted to ask God some hard questions or have wondered where God was during your heartache, illness, or loved one's death. It is the question Mary and Martha ask when their brother Lazarus dies. Jesus didn't explain things to them, but he asked if Martha believed (John 11:40).

In the book of Job, God answers Job out of the silence and explains all the many ways he has revealed his loving heart. "*Has the rain a father, or who has begotten the drops of dew? From whose womb did the ice come forth, and who has given birth to the frost of heaven?*" (38:28–29). God defends his love as if to say, "Observe all the ways I have loved and cared for you." Behind the scenes, God orchestrates everything for our good (Romans 8:28). Yet we often accuse him of silence.

Reflect

What steps can you take today to "trouble deaf heaven" with your deepest needs?

WEEK *four*

ARRIVING AT WISDOM

> We experience God's blessings in abundance the more we know, trust, and walk with him.

"The Lord blessed the latter days of Job more than his beginning."

JOB 42:12

DAY

GOD'S CALLING

READ JOB 39

C. S. Lewis once wrote, "It is to be expected that God's creation should be, for the large part, unintelligible to us." We are not meant to understand all that God created, Lewis explains, and despite our best scientific efforts, the Lord will always know more about his creation than we do.[1] God created all living things with purpose, and in chapter 39, he commends the animals for living up to this high calling. He describes how the mountain goat, the wild donkey, the ostrich, the horse, and the hawk all use instinct to grow strong in the wild, catch a scent of battle, or build a nest. God has wired them perfectly for their tasks. He has wired humans to seek joy, share life, and appreciate God's beauty.

God asks Job, "*Will you depend on him (the ox) because his strength is great, and will you leave to him your labor?*" (Job 39:11). In effect, God is asking, "Can you leave things up to me?" While we long to know all the things that God knows, we cannot see the future. The Holy Spirit can teach us to discern God's will and rest in God's sovereignty. We can acknowledge his providence and depend on his Word.

You may wonder what your calling is or how to discover it. Amazingly, you can start here in Job. To find our path, we must first find God. One of our vocations on earth is to seek eternity, or more specifically—to give birth to things that contribute to eternal well-being. God calls us to love him for who he is, and he created man to reflect his image (Genesis 1:27). Animals

---

[1] Walter Hooper, ed. *C. S. Lewis: Readings for Reflection and Meditation* (San Francisco: Harper, 1992), 39.

know what to do by instinct, just as the eagle searches "*the rocky crag and stronghold*" to spy out his prey (Job 39:28). But God is calling you to a far greater and more majestic purpose: to reflect his Son in the world. "*Beloved, we are God's children now, and what we will be has not yet appeared; but we know that when he appears we shall be like him, because we shall see him as he is*" (1 John 3:2).

Reflect

How is God calling you to reflect his Son to others?

DAY twenty-three

WHO IS THE BEHEMOTH?

READ JOB 40

Most of us are perplexed by the story of the Behemoth, but according to rabbinic legend, this was a primeval chaos monster God created. Man will only be allowed to tame the Behemoth when Jesus reigns, and before that, the beast will wreak havoc. This image is not comforting, and God tells Job to "*dress for action like a man*" to face it (Job 40:7). In a metaphorical sense, the Behemoth represents any powerful beast in life that is difficult for us to overcome. Job admits that he is "*of small account*" before God and lays his hand on his mouth to listen (40:4).

Once again, Job must wrestle with God's intentions. Job knows that he cannot tackle the beast. In our struggle to overcome things we cannot face, we may feel tired, anxious, or defeated. However, our deepest, most troubling issues are not overwhelming to God. As God shapes and grows us, he brings us to a point where we can face many of the giants that once held sway in our lives. Some giants may be inward sins such as pride, arrogance, anger, and self-righteousness. Unhealthy emotions and behaviors are destructive to others. But we have the help of the Holy Spirit and the light of Christ in our inner being to put off these "behemoths" from our lives (Romans 7:24–25).

I have a dear friend who struggles with anger and bitterness from the traumas she experienced as a girl. As a teenager, she was ignored, so she learned to hide her true self. As an adult, her feelings of shame continued and dictated much of who she became. My friend's recent journey into deeper fellowship with God has helped her become more honest and capable of finding a vocation that suits her. One Scripture she holds to is 2 Timothy 1:7, "*God gave us a spirit not of fear but of power and love and self-control.*" She has wrestled with gaining self-control over her dependencies, and memorizing this Scripture has helped.

When God looks at us, he sees a life worth redeeming.

The Lord's power discovered through prayer can help us overcome the chaos and destructive forces in our lives.

Reflect

What giants are you facing today? Ask God for his strength to overcome the crippling behemoths in your life.

DAY twenty-four

HOOKING THE GREAT LEVIATHAN

READ JOB 41:1–13

In his final work of fiction, *The Old Man and the Sea,* Ernest Hemingway tells the story of Santiago, a Cuban fisherman who fights with a great marlin. Although he finally hooks the fish, Santiago is pulled by the marlin further out to sea and becomes wounded in the struggle. He spends days and nights on the ocean, but when he finally catches the giant fish, he cannot bring him to shore in one piece. When he arrives at his village with only the bones waffling in the wake, Santiago suffers the shame of defeat. He is exhausted and near death, and he confesses that the marlin has done him in—but as a worthy adversary and even a brother.[1]

Some literary scholars have seen the giant fish in Hemingway's novel as the mythic Leviathan. God created this great creature as an unforgiving and undaunted beast that we cannot tame. The Leviathan cannot be pierced with a hook, nor can he be made a pet. *"Can you draw out Leviathan with a fishhook?"* God asks Job (Job 41:1). *"Will you play with him as with a bird, or will you put him on a leash?"* (41:5). Like the fisherman in Hemingway's story, Job can wrestle against God's power—but he will only return exhausted and discouraged. The Leviathan has a heart of stone that we cannot spear, like a millstone at the bottom of the sea.

We may try and master things out of our reach—like solving others' problems, reforming a prodigal child, or fixing things that we feel we have

---

1   Ernest Hemingway, *The Old Man and the Sea* (New York: Scribner, 1952), 95.

done wrong. We keep trying to reconcile with someone whose heart is hard—but the more we strive, the harder it becomes. God offers us his solutions and guidance. Our response is not a glib or simplistic "God's got this," but a deep, confident trust in God as he reveals himself in his Word and strengthens us in his Spirit. When we try and tackle things on our own without God's help, our human pride takes over as we try to accomplish what only God can do. As we commit to honest prayer, we can hand these troubling issues over to God and trust him to provide wise answers.

Reflect

How can you stop wrestling and rest in God's sovereignty today?

DAY twenty-five
THE LOCUST

READ JOB 41:14–34

The prophet Joel warned Israel about an invasion of locusts that would descend like a swarm. The people of Israel had experienced these infestations many times, and the locusts became a metaphor for a fearsome and destructive army that would one day invade, "*like blackness spreading across the mountains*" (Joel 2:2 NIV). These mythic warriors had the appearance of horses and galloped like cavalry, with a deafening sound, "*as with the rumbling of chariots*" (2:5). Joel admonished the people to return to God in repentance and prayer. "*Rend your hearts and not your garments. Return to the LORD your God*" (2:13).

The Leviathan in Job is described like the locusts of Joel. His back is rows of shields that cannot be separated, and his mouth breathes out flame while his flesh sticks together. We are reminded of a dragon, a nightmare, or the devil himself. The Leviathan, in all his rage, is a symbol of the fallen Satan, whose intense wrath will not be silenced until the end of time. This beast can be compared to "*the devil who had deceived them was thrown into the lake of fire and sulfur where the beast...will be tormented day and night forever and ever*" (Revelation 20:10). The beast meets a final end, but for now, we are left with a dragon who roams the earth. Like Job, we must repent, pray, and acknowledge that there is a beast more powerful than ourselves that we cannot overcome by human will.

God's challenging speech reveals that he created this Leviathan and is well acquainted with his strength. We cannot launch into life unguarded and unprepared, because the earth is not a spiritual playground. As Christians, we walk into enemy territory each time we bear the witness of Christ in a fallen world. Our responses to life's challenges are an example to others, and we must arm ourselves with what we need to stay strong. Of the many lifelines Jesus has given us, prayer and knowing God's Word are two of the greatest. In

Ephesians 6:10–18, Paul shows us how to walk in the ways of God. "*Therefore, take up the whole armor of God, that you may be able to withstand in the evil day, and having done all, to stand firm*" (Ephesians 6:13). We can use a shield of faith, the Word of God, and Spirit-led prayer.

Reflect

How does prayer fortify you or give you a shield of faith?

DAY
twenty-six

DOES HE CALL MY NAME?

READ JOB 42:1–9

    Mary Magdalene is an inspiring, brave woman. I like to imagine her real life in ancient Palestine, and in my recent book, *Seven Brave Women*, I explain Mary's role as a woman who laid groundwork for the early church.[1] When she decided to follow Rabbi Jesus, Mary had to leave her home in Magdala, a tiny town on the western Galilean Sea. Her family would have disowned her for the radical decision to follow an itinerant rabbi and a band of men. Mary was the first to appear at the tomb the morning after Jesus's death, showing the depth of her courage. When Jesus speaks to her—"*Mary!*"— she recognizes him and falls at his feet, praying humbly. "*I have seen the Lord*" (John 20:16–20). Jesus has seen her, too, and calls her to her future.

    Job pleads for a mediator who will see and recognize him, and in due time, one will come. God hears Job's faithful testimony and rewards him by coming in-person to talk with him. In turn, Job will confess the Lord: "*I had heard of you by the hearing of the ear, but now my eye sees you*" (Job 42:5). Many generations later, we are allowed to cast our eyes on Jesus Christ, the ultimate Redeemer. By our confession of the reality of who Jesus is, we are healed. Job could not anticipate such fulfillment of his desire, but his hope for a redeemer laid a foundation for us. God defends Job in front of others: "*You have not spoken of me what is right, as my servant Job has*" (42:7). He calls Job by his name and anoints him for prayer: "*My servant Job shall pray*

---

[1]   Sally Lombardo, *Seven Brave Women* (Bloomington, IN: WestBow Press, 2021).

for you" (42:8). Job prays for his friends and will be part of their healing. God's invitations become Job's redemption, and Job is healed by the wounds he has endured.

God calls Job by name to designate his role as servant and leader. Likewise, God calls us by name today and blesses us with unique spiritual gifts. Look for the ways God is calling to you and creating desires that were not there before. Listen to how characters like Mary Magdalene and Job speak to you through God's Word.

Reflect

How do the final chapters of Job show you some ways God is calling you?

DAY
twenty-seven & twenty-eight

BLESSINGS FOR ALL ETERNITY

READ JOB 42:10–16

One day not long ago, I was visiting a neighborhood in San Antonio that I did not know well. The city had just been through an epic ice storm, and I chose to take a run along a tree-lined street to get a feel for how the neighborhood had recovered. As I ran, I noticed that some trees were bursting with green, vibrant new life, while others were brown and dry. I saw that this was true of the various houses as well—some had strong roofs and new windows, and some had crumbled. The storm had wreaked havoc on homes and landscapes, and dead things stood in stark contrast to what had survived. Trees with deep roots stood firm, and homes with strong roofs weathered the storm. The psalmist describes shallow roots that lead to ruin (Psalm 1:3–4), and Matthew describes a house built upon the rock (Matthew 7:24–25). As I ran, I pondered how to build my life upon the Rock and stay rooted to the Vine I know as Christ.

Job has remained rooted in his loyalty and faith. This last, reassuring narrative describes the many ways Job is restored. Job prays for his friends, and the Lord makes him prosperous; he is granted twice as much as he had before. Friends and family give Job a large measure of silver and a gold ring, and his flocks, sons, and daughters increase. Job is redeemed in a mighty way he did not expect. We picture Job happy and satisfied with the blessings of God. His abundant fulfillment foreshadows our restoration in Christ.

God blesses Job with a double portion of many things—many descendants, fruitful fields, and prosperous life, just as Christ blesses us with abundant love. God also gave Job the blessing of praying for others and caring for a flock of people under his wing. Rooted in his love of God, Job's blessings would carry through generations. Eternal blessings don't fade with societal trends, ice storms, or world events. They are *"imperishable, undefiled, and unfading"* (1 Peter 1:3–5).

Today, our heavenly blessings may look a lot like Job's—new family members, restored friendships, satisfying fellowship, or inspiring time spent in God's creation. They are moments when you worship God's faithfulness and communicate his love. You can praise God for opening your eyes to his Word (Psalm 119:18).

Reflect

Where do you see God's eternal blessings in your life? How can you share God's love and blessings with others?

WEEK *five*

GOD'S PROVIDENCE PROVIDES HOPE

God's providence directs us.

"Where you go I will go, and where you lodge I will lodge."

RUTH 1:16

DAY twenty-nine

DOES HE CALL MY NAME?

READ RUTH 1:1–5

    Change can be terrifying. Relocating homes and moving our families can take so much out of us, and our society does not recognize the emotional toll on a life rearranged. We often give ourselves little time to adjust to the inevitable discomfort. Recently my small group studied the book of Ruth, and we admired this young Bible hero's ability to embrace significant change. Ruth's choice to relocate meant leaving her culture, religious tradition, and family—everything familiar to her. She might never have visited Israel before or seen its rivers and hills. Ruth's decision to go must have been based on discernment and prayer, indicating a life with God that she already had. We will explore together how courage empowers her.

    Ruth's story highlights the sovereign purposes of God, first for a brave young woman and subsequently for generations to come. The Lord worked through Ruth and gave her courage, faithfulness, and loyalty to her mother-in-law Naomi, a grieving woman who makes the uncomfortable confession, "*I went away full, and the* LORD *has brought me back empty*" (Ruth 1:21). Since Naomi feels empty even when she is journeying with Ruth, our hero could have taken offense at this, but she does not. Ruth might have thought, "Does that mean I don't matter to you?" She might have struggled with a desire to turn and run! Instead, Ruth chooses to trust her knowledge of this Israelite God and what Yahweh supplies to those who follow. In short, Ruth allows herself to be chosen. According to author Kirsten Nielsen, "God himself chose

Ruth, just as he had chosen the patriarchs, Samuel, and David as king."[1] Ruth's journey was a divine appointment, accepted with intuition and faith. We, too, can have the courage to follow God's path on a remarkable journey of faith. The apostle Paul reminds us of our source of strength: "*So we are always of good courage…for we walk by faith, not by sight*" (2 Corinthians 5:6–7).

Reflect

How might God be inviting you into a different way to pray or new type of devotion to his Word?

---

[1] Kirsten Nielsen, *Ruth—A Commentary* (Louisville, KY: John Knox Press, 1997), 1–2.

DAY

NAOMI OR MARA?

READ RUTH 1:6–14

Have you ever explored the meaning of your name? In many cultures, names have vital importance. Greek culture has a custom of naming a firstborn child after the father, and other cultures have similar traditions. Names can also become part of how we see our future. For example, Jacob was renamed when he asked the angel to bless him. His given name became *Israel*, for his descendants would be God's people and provide his purpose (Genesis 32:24–32). My given name is Sarah, which in Hebrew means "princess."[1] As an adult, I grew into a sense of obligation to live up to a name that signifies worth and dignity before God.

Likewise, Naomi's name has meaning and reflects her journey with God. Naomi means "pleasant or sweet."[2] However, in the first chapter of Ruth, this strong woman is depressed and bitter. When we meet her, she blames her sadness on the hand of the Lord, as we sometimes do. When Naomi returns to her beloved country, she tells her neighbors, *"Call me Mara [bitter], for the Almighty has dealt very bitterly with me"* (Ruth 1:20). Naomi may have let her true feelings show to gain attention and pity, but God will use her daughter-in-law's commitment and choices to change Naomi's self-pity into gratitude. Naomi continues to call on God, using his personal and covenant name Yahweh, to display her underlying faith that God will not abandon her. With God's

---

1   "Sarah," in *The Exhaustive Concordance of the Bible*, ed. James Strong (Cincinnati: Jennings & Graham, 1890).
2   "Mara," in *International Standard Bible Encyclopedia*, ed. James D. Orr (Peabody, MA: Hendrickson Publishers, 1915).

help, she matures into her chosen name and assumes the role of a helper and friend. God stays with us and teaches us as long as we need, too.

Ultimately, we must choose what kind of name and attitude we will assume. God offers us this freedom. If your past makes you feel bitter, hopeless, or stuck, it is wise to seek God's healing rather than name yourself *Mara*. A wise woman and teacher I know once suggested asking God to rename you with a new, personal, and spiritual name. This spiritual exercise allows God to call you with more clarity and purpose. Once I took a personal retreat in the mountains to ask God for this same blessing, and he provided two beautiful names. I looked up these stories in the Bible, and to this day, I love thinking of one aspect of myself as "Deborah." I hope and pray that I can live like her image, "*like the sun as it rises in its might*" (Judges 5:31 NRSV).

Reflect

If you are a Christian, God calls you by name (Romans 8:28–30). How does this calling give you hope?

DAY thirty-one

WHAT IS LOYALTY?

READ RUTH 1:15–22

Loyalty is an unsung hero. People who are loyal to family, spouse, and friends are not always applauded for their steadfastness, as trends change and individualist culture expands. Lifelong loyalty can even be seen as a weakness of character or an inability to stand up for one's rights. Yet devotion often requires sacrifice, and God commends this. When Jesus explains to his followers that he is *"the bread that came down from heaven,"* many become confused and rethink their loyalty (John 6:58–66). It was hard for first-century followers, especially devout Jews, to stand firm with this unexpected Messiah. Jesus asks the Twelve if they will leave him, but Peter responds: *"Lord, to whom shall we go? You have the words of eternal life"* (John 6:68). I have reflected on these words many times when faced with life choices.

Our loyalty matters, as do our choices. Naomi's other daughter-in-law, Orpah, decides to go back to her people and her gods because that is where her loyalty lies. Ruth makes a different choice, and her dedication to God blesses many. She steps out and seeks a path with God, announcing, *"Where you go I will go, and where you lodge I will lodge. Your people shall be my people, and your God my God"* (Ruth 1:16). We wonder how Ruth develops such allegiance since she has never even been to Naomi's homeland. Just as in our previous devotional, the answer may come from the significance of a name.

Ruth makes her way with Naomi to Bethlehem. The author's choice of Bethlehem is not accidental, as its meaning is literally "house of bread."[1] The two women are looking for sustenance, assurance, and literal nourishment, just as the disciples looked to Jesus for a reason to stay under his tutelage and care. They were dependent on Jesus for guidance and patronage for support. Jesus described himself as *"the bread of God...who comes down from heaven and gives life to the world"* (John 6:33). Ruth and Naomi are also looking for God's bread. They arrive at the time of the barley harvest, looking for food and a purpose for their lives. When the story ends, the harvest is ripe. Their faith in God and loyalty to one another will guide them as they reap what providence has sown.

Reflect

Read Philippians 2:5–11. Who is the greatest example of loyalty? How does his example make our loyalty possible?

---

[1] "Bethlehem," in *International Standard Bible Encyclopedia*.

DAY

DOES DIVINE APPOINTMENT EXIST?

READ RUTH 2:1–7

Sometimes we have occasions of serendipity in life, when an event happens by chance in a surprisingly beneficial way. We often refer to these as coincidences, and they look like running into an old friend, arriving somewhere in just the nick of time, or pursuing a long-awaited dream. Recently, a childhood friend in crisis whom I had not seen for years called my house. She has experienced health challenges and significant loss, and for some reason, my name kept popping into her head. In just a few days, we began a friendship based on mutual encouragement and the words of Christ. I thank God often for the serendipity of our encounter and God's hand in our lives.

Ruth and Boaz cross each other's paths out in a field. Given Boaz's work, the meeting between a slave girl and a wealthy landowner was quite unlikely. Their chance meeting quickly makes itself known to Naomi as a divine appointment, and she takes the initiative to help Ruth see this too. Ruth knew little of Hebrew customs, but she trusted Naomi's love and care and listened to her advice. In Hebrew culture, the family unit was a top priority. Alongside loyalty to God and allegiance to his people, family, and property in Israel were where God kept his covenant promises to his people. Family and property were central, as clans protected and rescued people of their family lines.[1]

Ruth may or may not have seen her meeting with Boaz as a divine

---

[1] David Atkinson, *The Message of Ruth: The Wings of Refuge*. vol. 9 of *The Bible Speaks Today*, ed. J. A. Motyer and John R. W. Stott (Downers Grove, IL: InterVarsity Press, 1985), 57.

encounter, but the subsequent events would have shown her that God's favor was working behind the scenes. God works behind the scenes in our lives, too. As we pray for such direction, God guides us in our choices, so *"the Spirit helps us in our weakness, interceding for us with groans too deep for words.... And we know that for those who love God all things work together for good, for those who are called according to his purpose"* (Romans 8:26–28). When we listen and follow, we are invited to be part of God's larger plan of bringing the kingdom, just as Ruth was.

Reflect

Describe a moment of divine coincidence in your life. How does this help you trust in God's love?

DAY thirty-three

GOD USES US IN UNEXPECTED WAYS

READ RUTH 2:8–16

God gives grace in unexpected places and uses our lives in creative ways. This was the case in the story of Esther, a young Hebrew girl who became queen of Persia. Esther had no idea that her insignificant, humble voice would convince the king to rescue her people (Esther 4:13–14). The gift of unexpected rescue was also a theme in Joseph's life. During thirteen long years in prison, Joseph learned to interpret dreams, which led him through despair and misfortune to eventually become governor of Egypt, the pharaoh's right-hand man (Genesis 41:37–46). When we allow our lives to be open to God's leading, he will provide protection, guidance, and unanticipated opportunities for places and people we can serve.

Ruth follows Naomi's advice to the place where she "*happened to come to the part of the field belonging to Boaz*" (Ruth 2:3). This man from Bethlehem transforms Ruth from a somewhat isolated, marginalized, and insignificant Moabite woman to someone of worth and dignity. Did this happen by chance, or was it because Ruth said yes to God, offering him a willing heart? Ruth is given a new role and purpose as she trusts God and follows his leading even into a threshing house. Jesus provides the same offer to an isolated and outcast woman on a dusty road beside a well. Although she is a Samaritan, he speaks to her with tender care and offers the promise of living water if she will repent and turn. Surprised, this woman welcomes Jesus's counsel about her need to change and dares to run and tell others all she has learned (John 4:7–29). Both Ruth and the woman and the well were blessed because they trusted God's mercy and love.

Sometimes we, too, are on a long road that seems misdirected or unfulfilling. When we pray for guidance, God hears us and offers us unanticipated, creative ways to work and serve that only he can provide. He gives us chance encounters that turn into blessings. Ruth and Boaz together find a new way forward; they promise each other happiness—but each will choose to let go of a former path and turn toward a new life. Ruth leaves her people. Boaz gives himself permission to take a foreigner for a wife. He offers Ruth protection, inviting her to "*be richly rewarded by the LORD, the God of Israel, under whose wings you have come to take refuge*" (Ruth 2:12 NIV). God invites them both into unexpected, new life.

Reflect

Where do you see God inviting you to trust him in a different way?

DAY *thirty-four*

THE POWER TO BLESS

READ RUTH 2:17–23

People can disappoint us. In all our relationships over a lifetime, family and friends will betray us or say things that hurt. It can be hard to pray honestly for others and even harder to forgive them. We may be ashamed of our responses, or we may be reluctant to admit the truth of what occurred. Thankfully, the Bible has examples of blessings we can pray when we just don't know what to say. Throughout the years, I have prayed specific blessings over my children and asked the Lord to help them grow in character. For instance, Proverbs 7:1–2 advises, "*My son, keep my words and treasure my commandments with you; keep my commandments and live, keep my teaching as the apple of your eye.*" In God's mysterious ways, his blessings can call out the good.

Myron Madden writes that we cannot begin to measure the far-reaching effects of a blessing. "We cannot earn a blessing; it is given by pure goodwill, and this is the fact that dispels the curse of a broken law."[1] Madden's book is appropriately titled *The Power to Bless*. God chooses to bless us abundantly in his Word, such as the gracious blessing Moses prayed as the Hebrews entered their promised land: "*The LORD bless you and keep you; the LORD make his face to shine upon you and be gracious to you*" (Numbers 6:24–25). Naomi knew this prayer and chose to bless Boaz in a similar way after Ruth spent the day in the fields. Naomi prayed, "'*May [Boaz] be blessed by the LORD, whose kindness has not forsaken the living or the dead!' Naomi also*

---

[1] Myron Madden, *The Power to Bless* (Insight Press, Inc., 1999), 120.

said to her, 'This man is a close relative of ours, one of our redeemers'" (Ruth 2:20). These powerful words were the first mention of a kinsman-redeemer, a concept with layers of meaning.

We looked at the term kinsman-redeemer in the book of Job. The Deuteronomic Law said that a man's brother or nearest kin was to redeem the widow of his relative and marry her (Deuteronomy 25:5). Blessing Boaz as the guardian-redeemer would have done what Myron Madden suggests—break the curse of human death and give far-reaching effects to a family. As evidence this has occurred, Ruth becomes the mother to Obed, whose lineage will bear King David and later Jesus's earthly father, Joseph. Blessings play out in many ways, and their power is still ours to use today.

Reflect

How can you bless someone today with kind words and the love of God? Pray that you will see the results with God's help.

DAY thirty-five

THE BIBLICAL TYPE SCENE

READ RUTH 1–2

As you read through your Bible, you may notice that some stories seem to repeat themselves. The characters, setting, or plot may vary, but the overall scene is the same. These stories are referred to as *type scenes*, a term first coined in literature and later applied to biblical study by Robert Alter. A type scene is an archetypal moment that can take the form of a betrothal, conception, or announcement. The moment does not just happen by chance but always has a more significant theological meaning. Some of these scenes include Abraham's visit from an angel before Sarah's conception, Isaac's meeting Rebecca at the well, Jacob's first sighting of Rachel at the same well, and Mary's visitation by an angel telling her of Jesus's birth. Ruth and Boaz's meeting is a type scene similar to Isaac and Rebecca at the well. Here, water is used for anointing and a blessing of hope.

When Boaz acknowledges that Ruth has left home, he comments on her brave journey of faith (Ruth 2:11). Ruth left Moab just as the patriarchs left their country. Boaz offers her water as a source of new life and extends his protection—leading to betrothal, marriage, and birth. Ruth is like an archetypal Abraham, who "goes forth from the land and a father's house," and her journey to Canaan makes her a "kind of matriarch by adoption," says Robert Alter.[1] Just as Rachel drew water for Jacob at the well in Hebron, Boaz drew water for Ruth as a pledge. Ruth's marriage connects her to the matriarchs Sarah, Leah, Rebekah, and Rachel. Additionally, Ruth is an alien and not a Hebrew,

---

[1] Robert Alter, *The Art of the Biblical Narrative* (Downers Grove, IL: IVP, 2016), 56.

proving that she stands for others who will be grafted into the people of God. Such a prototype foreshadows the path that Jesus will take to open God's promise of life to the Gentiles. Type scenes reveal the larger will of God.

    Ruth's long journey to Judah carried no guarantee of success, but she knew enough about Yahweh through her former husband's family to trust God through significant change. Our lives may take unforeseen turns, and sometimes we wonder why we are headed down a specific path. I often find myself stopping along the path and hoping I am still following God. I find, however, that if I pray and ask God to use me in his larger will, my road opens up, and I start to walk again.

Reflect

Like God chose Ruth, how might he be choosing you to be used for his work?

WEEK *six*

IN
ALL
THINGS,
GOD
IS
WORKING
FOR
OUR
GOOD

> God works all things together for good for those who love him.

"Blessed be the Lord, who has not left you this day without a redeemer."

RUTH 4:14

DAY thirty-six

THE LEVIRATE LAW AND THE GO'EL

READ RUTH 3:1–6

How should we begin to understand the concept of a kinsman-redeemer? In Ruth 3–4, the author links two ancient customs—the law of levirate marriage and the law of the Go'el. *Levir* means brother-in-law, and levirate marriage laws protected a woman when the man of the house had died. It also ensured that the family clan would live on. The other custom described is the law of the *Go'el*, a protector or kinsman whose duty it was to redeem. This buy-back applied to obtaining land, monetary inheritance, or property of any kind—including a wife. The *Go'el* was a man who even supported family members who had become slaves. Ruth's work gleaning wheat on the fringes of the fields indicates that she held the status of a servant in need of protection.[1]

How does this apply to us? Life with God means that we respect and love our families, and we take kinship to heart in ways that look different for each culture. We honor God by respecting boundaries and taking on responsibility, especially toward the older people in our care and the church communities we love. Naomi assumed the role of Ruth's parent. She prayed for her, listened for God's direction, and eventually counseled her to meet Boaz at the threshing floor, even when this seemed illogical. Ruth may have hesitantly approached the wealthy man's barn that night, but when she arrived at the threshing floor, she would have seen reapers tossing harvested grain into the strong evening winds. As the wind blew away the outer husks, pure

---

1   Atkinson, *The Message of Ruth*, 91–92.

seed remained—a beautiful sight. Although Ruth could not see the larger narrative of her story, the threshing was a picture of her own refinement; she was to be part of bearing Israel's seed. Though a humble servant, Ruth was God's choice to change a family line.

Reflect

For whom can you act in the role of kinsman, helper, and friend?

DAY thirty-seven

GOD KEEPS ME SAFE

READ RUTH 3:7–13

There is a beautiful poem titled "The Wings of Refuge" printed in the front of a commentary on Ruth. I was comforted with how well this poem describes her journey. It may apply to your life, as it depicts how we look for rest in God. The first section is a lament, but the poem's final words end in discovery and joy.

> And after all,
> I find myself at this oasis—an unlooked-for harbor, a refuge.
> I had no hope, but turning back along the path I came,
> I see a gracious hand and loving smile.
> I see a guiding light and feel a protecting wing.
> My tears have turned to jewels and my bitterness to honey.
> Keep me, O Lord, safe—in the refuge of your wings.[1]

In a world of unsettling and constant change, we too might welcome a "guiding light and protecting wing." We are afraid to emerge from a place of safety to a place of new adventure and change. By chapter 3, Ruth has gone out from Naomi's protection, but she will make a pleasant discovery about God. He has followed her and provided for her welfare, even away from her former covering. The corner of Boaz's garment that will cover her is the covenant family of Yahweh, and now she stands ready to play her

---

1   Atkinson, *The Message of Ruth*, 29–30.

part as daughter.[2] "*Who are you?*" Boaz asks. "'*I am your servant Ruth,*' she said. '*Spread the corner of your garment over me, since you are a guardian-redeemer of our family.*'" (Ruth 3:9 NIV).

Other Bible heroes toss their garments onto others, symbolizing a transfer of God's favor, a mantle of grace. Elijah passes his cloak to Elisha, who asks for "*a double portion*" of his spirit when Elijah is taken away (2 Kings 2:9). When God chooses Ezekiel, he says, "*I spread the corner of my garment over you...and enter into covenant with you*" (Ezekiel 16:8). When God's favor returns to Israel, he bequeaths them "*a garment of praise instead of a spirit of despair*" (Isaiah 61:3 NIV). The point is that God continues to cover us with his provision and protection. We can trust that as we step out to find a new identity in Christ, a new calling, and a greater purpose, we are covered by his grace.

Reflect

Can you remember a time when you were afraid, but you felt God's presence and protection?

---

[2] Atkinson, *The Message of Ruth*, 101.

DAY thirty-eight

DOES GOD HAVE A PLAN FOR MY LIFE?

READ RUTH 3:14–18

One afternoon I sat with a friend on her front porch, and we discussed the many places where she had lived around the world. Some were beautiful vacation spots with mountains and lakes, and some were urban centers. Back in the small town where we first met, my friend said she felt safe at home again. She was content. "I'm still worried about one thing, though," she confessed. "Do you think God has a plan for my life? Have I messed it up by moving around everywhere?" While we all search for God's ways, I believe he has a "super-plan" that includes just our formation and growth in him. God's will is that we take on his character in Christ.

I love to read the promises of God in the Old Testament. The repeated theme—that God knows and loves his people—gives me comfort and hope. Jeremiah prophecies that God will bring his people home and rescue them. I have sent this verse to my children, and I often repeat it in my work as a chaplain: "*For I know the plans I have for you, declares the LORD, plans for your welfare and not for evil, to give you a future and a hope*" (Jeremiah 29:11). Throughout Ruth, Yahweh has a plan, a meta-narrative that man cannot thwart. He brings Ruth and Naomi to the harvest of bread and a new family line. Barrenness and bitterness lead to fulfillment. Ruth begins with famine but ends with birth. There is a "reversal of female fortune" that overcomes the emptiness of the past and restores the fullness of life to the present.[1]

God's specific plans may not be outlined on a daily planner as we

---

1   Nielsen, *Ruth*, 10.

would like, but his will can be found in his Word. For one, God intends the fruit of the Spirit to be formed in us, and he will provide opportunities to grow this fruit in our lives. These occasions will include both joy and sorrow, since we learn best when we need God most. "*Love, joy, peace, patience, kindness, goodness, faithfulness, gentleness, [and] self-control*" are all part of God's plan in our lives (Galatians 5:22–23). Ruth moves forward patiently with joy, hope, and kindness. Her goodness and love keep her story alive.

Reflect

Read Matthew 12:33 and John 15:5. Is your life bearing fruit?

DAY thirty-nine

UNSANDALED

READ RUTH 4:1–10

When my children were growing up, we had a nightly shoe collection. I asked the kids to find the shoes they had left by the side door, in front of the couch, or under the dining table. Their ragged sneakers and ballet shoes served as telltale signs of where they had been during the day, and I knew whose shoes belonged to whom. If they failed to take those discarded tennis shoes back to the closet, I would toss them on the porch. The shoe collection was a reminder that we all have responsibilities.

In ancient times, the sandal was a mark of trust. Its worn nature indicated where someone had walked on his journey and what his value was to society. Even John the Baptist warned the Pharisees: "*I baptize you with water for repentance, but he who is coming after me is mightier than I, whose sandals I am not worthy to carry*" (Matthew 3:11). John memorialized even the sandals of the Lord. The mark of the sandal proved that shoes carried weight.

In Ruth 4, we find Boaz asking the other nearest relative if he will be redeeming Ruth, the Moabite woman. Boaz must first buy Naomi's land; then, he can acquire Ruth as his wife and provide a male heir. An unknown, closer kinsman has a chance to redeem, but he declines his right according to the levirate law. As a sign, he draws off his sandal, tosses it in the ring, and gives it to Boaz (Ruth 4:8). Interestingly, Deuteronomic Law said that such a man would not be respected; *"That man's line shall be known in Israel as The Family of the Unsandaled"* (Deuteronomy 25:10 NIV). The phrase may sound strange to us, but in Boaz's time, it meant that the man had assumed collective shame. We can assume that God had providentially chosen Boaz for Ruth, so the responsibility goes to the man God selects.

We need to be willing to take on responsibility for what God calls us to do. Think about your own paths with God and the symbolic shoes you wear. Sometimes our shoes will pick up mud, when we walk alongside another person through a painful and messy season. Other times, our calling can take us into deep water, and our shoes get water-logged and need to be hung out to dry. There are also times when worn shoes call us to rest. Along each path, we can remember the way Jesus walked for us—up to Calvary, to pay a price far greater than his sandal.

Reflect

Where are you willing to travel with God, even with muddy shoes?

DAY

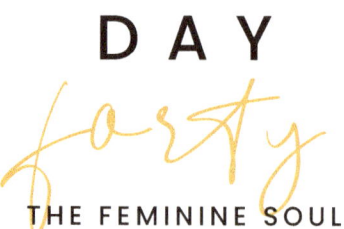

THE FEMININE SOUL

READ RUTH 4:10–12

A friend of mine wrote an excellent book entitled *The Feminine Soul*. In her intuitive writing, Janet Davis explores the uniquely feminine perspective that God gives to women. She describes women in the Bible who dared to speak up, be honest, embrace their vulnerability, and reach out to Jesus to grow in faith. The book encourages women to be present to their whole selves—physically, emotionally, spiritually, and intellectually. When we do so, we can be honest with God and find deeper connection. She explains how Ruth and Naomi "honored their desire to experience God in all of life by learning the art of listening to his voice in intuitive ways."[1] These insights showed me two lessons from Ruth's character.

First, honesty with God requires courage. We don't have evidence of how Ruth prayed when her husband died, but we can imagine that her prayers were filled with sadness and frustration: "Why did you let that happen, Lord? Now what should I do?" Her desperate need for help called her into honest prayer, and her openness to God's answer called her to follow him on a new path. God directed Ruth to things she didn't recognize, but she listened to God's voice with her heart and followed him with her actions. Her cries for hope are not unlike the questions I hear on hospital floors and in patients' rooms. God offers us hope; he calls us to be his children.

God's provision doesn't always look like what we think. As a young woman, Ruth probably never imagined that she would lose her husband and

---

1   Janet Davis, *The Feminine Soul* (Colorado Springs: NavPress, 2006), 176.

live with her mother-in-law. She probably did not aspire to be a servant and gleaner in a field, nor did she expect to marry an older man who adhered to the Deuteronomic code. Yet, in all of these changing circumstances, Ruth trusted in God's provision, kept praying, and continued walking toward the unfolding of his will. Her willingness to be vulnerable and trust her knowledge of God were attitudes that invited blessing.

Reflect

How can honest prayer help you trust God's provision in your life?

DAY
forty-one

MARRIAGE, PARTNERSHIP, AND HOPE

READ RUTH 4:13–22

According to theologian and writer Dietrich Bonhoeffer, "Marriage is more than just having love for one another. It has a higher dignity and power and is God's great ordinance. You see only the heaven of your happiness, but you act as a post of responsibility towards mankind."[1] I like this quote as a description of the marriage of Boaz and Ruth. Their union is like an umbrella that will cover a long line of Hebrews loyal to God. Their son is part of the ancestry of David and the family line of Jesus. Today, God still uses marriage as an example of his love for us. He uses our sacred commitments as examples of his faithfulness.

The final chapter of Ruth is like a happy ending that we read about in fairy tales. Boaz loves Ruth, God gives her a son, and the women praise Naomi for the faithful guardian-redeemer: "*He will renew your life and sustain you in old age*" (Ruth 4:15 NIV). We wonder how things worked out so well. There has been a rescue, a conception, and a boy who will now be famous in Israel, sustaining his family into old age. We might be tempted to say: "I guess things don't always work out like this today." But the good news is that they do! "*For all the promises of God find their Yes in him. That is why it is through him that we utter our Amen to God for his glory*" (2 Corinthians 1:20).

Jesus is the unexpected Son given by God; he is our true Kinsman-Redeemer who bought us back from death and sin, and he renews and sustains us for life ahead, even into old age. He is the bridegroom who is betrothed to

---

1   Quoted in Lewis Smedes, *Sex in the Real World* (Lion Press, 1976), 176.

the church and believers forever. He is our happy ending.

The church is the bride of Christ. As believers, we carry the Spirit in our hearts and invite him into our relationships and witness. Like Ruth, we can tell the story of our rescue, or, like Naomi, we can tell others how God brought us from bitterness and lack of hope to joy and fulfillment. *"As the bridegroom rejoices over the bride, so shall your God rejoice over you"* (Isaiah 62:5). Let this prophecy give you hope in your union with God and with those you love.

Reflect

How is God blessing you through your Bible study and prayer—with new friends, clearer purpose, or a closer walk with God?

DAY forty-two

JOY IN SUFFERING

READ RUTH 1–4

I have a friend who led a Bible study in a maximum-security prison while she was also a professor at Yale. At the Yale Center for Faith and Culture, Angela Gorrell worked on a project called "Theology of Joy and the Good Life," where she taught about joy and a life worth living. In her recent book, Gorrell shares her journey away from the pain of losing family members and towards newfound joy. During the months of the prison study and the relationships built within, Gorrell awakened to the fact that great joy can exist alongside sorrow and suffering. While listening to the women's stories of resilience, she began to develop a "concept of making pain productive without justifying or glorifying suffering." Against all logic, she began to see the true "work of joy" in the middle of crises of faith and belief.[1]

Ruth is a person who has found joy in the middle of her suffering. Unlike the book of Job, suffering is not a significant theme in Ruth, nor is the silence of God a major issue. None of the characters wrestle with God's leading or rail at God about life's misfortunes. Naomi, Ruth, Boaz, and the village elders have a sense of deep acceptance and satisfaction. I would suggest that this is because they believe that joy is possible. When we anticipate that God has joy in store and know that God's promises are true, our disappointments and sorrow take on greater weight, and they can be productive. For instance, we can decide to use our suffering for good, and we learn that finding joy is in part up to us. Ruth may have looked for joy on

---

1 Angela Gorrell, *The Gravity of Joy* (Grand Rapids, MI: Eerdmans, 2021), 96.

the face of Boaz when he saw her in the field. She may have looked for joy on the threshing floor and embraced it. She remembered the simple concept of gratitude.

Joy is not elusive, nor is it hard to grasp. Inevitably, life will not lead us down all the paths we hoped for, but we can walk the paths we're on with joy. We can find joy in David's Psalms and in Ruth's marriage story. We can celebrate joy when a child grows and matures. God has created a desire for eternity in our hearts and a longing for joy. Can you see it just in front of you?

Reflect

Where can you look for joy today? List three ways God is present to you in the middle of a struggle.

WEEK *seven*

THE DIFFICULT PROCESS OF ASKING GOD

> We can pour out our souls to the Lord, and he will answer.

"For this child I prayed, and the Lord has granted me my petition that I made to him."

1 SAMUEL 1:27

DAY forty-three

HANNAH OPENS HER HEART

READ RUTH 1:1–11

    The birth of Samuel is a story of a woman opening her life to be used by God. Hannah longs for a child, and she makes a vow promising to give this child to the Lord. Her Spirit-filled prayer and Samuel's birth are a type scene of God's anointing.[1] Hannah prays, and God remembers her and fulfills her desire, but in his time and for his larger purpose. The birth of Samuel will provide a second Exodus for Israel, from chaos into order. Hannah seeks God in the midst of despair, and God responds with more than she could ask or imagine.

    Hannah's story is full of irony. She and Elkanah visit the temple during the Festival of Tabernacles to receive harvest blessings, but Hannah has no crop or child of her own. Her awareness of lack would have been acutely painful. The couple is from Ramah, a town later cited by Jeremiah as the place of Herod's massacre. In contrast to such death, Hannah's faith will bring a son to govern Israel and create new life. Hannah's name itself means "favor and grace," which God provides in abundance.[2] Before this favor occurs, Hannah seeks God through tears and a willingness to be part of a bigger plan. Without a desire to open her heart, Hannah would have been stuck in self-pity, as we often can be. Her acceptance of God's greater plan, the larger narrative, becomes part of her healing and hope.

---

1   See Day 35 for a definition of type scenes.
2   "Hannah," in *International Standard Bible Encyclopedia,* ed. James D. Orr (Peabody, MA: Hendrickson Publishers, 1915).

There are few sources of pain so deep as the unfulfilled desire for a child. God allows Hannah to struggle, but when she cries out in prayer, he meets her with strength. We may long for many things—for restored relationships, for a wayward child to come home, or for a greater purpose and calling. We can trust God to hear our prayers. The story of Hannah shows that true intimacy with God can fill our hearts and bear fruit that only he can produce. Hannah takes her great heartache to the altar. We often think that if God meets our requests, then our lives will be made right, and we will finally be happy. But God counsels us to seek him and find fulfillment: "*Seek first the kingdom of God and his righteousness, and all these things will be added to you*" (Matthew 6:33).

Reflect

What are you longing for in life? Can you be honest about your desires and let God fill them in his way?

DAY forty-four

FROM DESPERATION TO PRAYER

READ RUTH 1:6–11

First Samuel 1 is a startling passage. Peninnah has children, God's favor, and Elkanah's attention, yet she provokes Hannah out of jealousy—a dominant theme in Bible texts. Jealousy rears its head when money, favor, or inheritance are involved. Stories of jealous pairs—such as Sarah and Hagar, Cain and Abel, and Jacob and Esau—demonstrate how envy destroys relationships and deters fruitfulness. Peninnah has provoked Hannah "*year by year*," so much that Hannah "*wept and would not eat*" (1 Samuel 1:7).

Yet Hannah's heartache is not just from Peninnah's treatment. Her weeping comes from the fear that she will never have a child and the feeling that God has abandoned her. If we have prayed for something that never comes, we know her emotional pain. Hannah's description, "*She was deeply distressed...and wept bitterly*" (1:10), is accurately translated as "exceedingly bitter." This is how Naomi describes herself, too (Ruth 1:13). Elkanah wonders why Hannah is so sad and why his love and attention are insufficient. "*Am I not more to you than ten sons?*" (1 Samuel 1:8).

Desperation can drive us to say and do things we might not normally say. It can motivate us to pursue God or to reject him. Hannah has had enough of sorrow and pain, and she bravely starts to take action. "*Hannah rose*," verse 9 says. She pushes back from the table to make her way to the temple, where she will pray aloud, pour out her grief, and beg God to have mercy on her sorrow. She makes a vow, a bargain with God, and promises to do her part if God will do his. Deep longing can drive us to honest prayer. "*If you will indeed look on the affliction of your servant and...give to your servant a son*," Hannah pleads, "*then I will give him to the LORD for all the days of his life*" (1:11). She makes a promise to God, and God honors it.

Hannah was tormented in many ways. We, too, have seasons of pain, and we may move from denial and grief to anger. We beg God to take something away or restore what was lost. Ultimately, when our efforts bring little fruit, we learn to release our own will. Our prayers may not be answered as we want them to be, but we can take heart knowing that God hears us.

Reflect

What are your deepest needs? How can you trust that God hears your prayers? *"Answer me when I call, O God of my righteousness! You have given me relief when I was in distress"* (Psalm 4:1).

DAY forty-five

FINDING YOUR VOICE

READ RUTH 1:11–18

How often do we make promises that endure for *"all the days"* of life (1 Samuel 1:11)? Not often, I would suggest. The closest we get is probably a wedding vow, but Hannah tells another story. Her vow to give her baby son to the Lord for his whole life is sanctified as she says, *"no razor shall touch his head,"* promising loyalty to a Nazarite vow (1:11). It is the same vow God required of Samson, a judge who delivered Israel (Judges 14). Such a man could not drink or eat from a grapevine, cut his hair, or go near a dying person. It was no small oath.

In our reading today, Hannah is confronted by the temple priest, who criticizes her because her lips are moving in prayer, but her voice is inaudible. Eli accuses her of being drunk: *"Put your wine away from you!"* (1 Samuel 1:14). His command is ironic since Hannah has just pledged to raise her son in the sober Nazarite lifestyle. Maybe Hannah was praying in the Spirit, who was forming in her the right words to pray; maybe she was hiding her words for fear they would be misunderstood. Nonetheless, Hannah defends herself boldly: *"No, my lord! I am a woman troubled in spirit…pouring out my soul before the LORD"* (1:15). At this moment, Hannah finds her voice and testifies to her dependence on God and trust in God's plan for her son. Her statement may have even surprised her! Yet Hannah's moment of honesty pivots the story toward hope and healing.

To find our voice, we must face our fears and be open to God's new direction. Maybe you are afraid of changing a destructive life pattern or ending a difficult relationship. Maybe there is a new line of work you should pursue or a new job you should consider. With God's strength, *"speaking the truth in love, we are to grow up in all aspects into him who is the Head, even Christ"* (Ephesians 4:15 NASB). Growing up is never easy, but we can take heart from Hannah's courage and the testimony of God's work in her life. She must have been surprised at the power of her voice and the strength she had discovered during her time of prayer.

Reflect

How has prayer changed you or given you courage to find your voice?

DAY
forty-six

HANNAH'S JOY

READ RUTH 1:18–20

Among other things, I am a doula and natural childbirth instructor. This was an unexpected vocation but one that brings me great joy. I have spent rich and beautiful moments with young moms and families I would not have known otherwise. Being a doula with a woman in labor is like being granted access to joy. A doula—a birth advocate or companion—is a role of support, nurture, and friendship. Doulas understand the emotions of birth mothers and recognize their fears and needs for validation. Pregnancy and childbirth are life-giving seasons.

The hard part about my role as a doula is that sometimes I must walk with families through miscarriage, disappointment, or infertility, just as Hannah faced. Many women navigate these difficult roads. At the time of her prayer, Hannah does not know the outcome, as we do when we read the end of her story. She simply offers up her aching heart and makes a promise about the child she hopes to bear—that she will train him up in the knowledge and love of God. Thankfully, God has given us an example of a woman who prayed, trusted, and waited.

Hannah names her baby *shemu'el*, meaning "name of God." By changing a few letters in Hebrew, his name also means *sha'ul me'el*, translated as "asked of God."[1] Hannah asked God for this child, waited for God's response, and followed his will for her life. This is the mystery of prayer. Alongside our hope to receive a desired outcome, we must be willing to hear what the Spirit

---

1   "Samuel," in *International Standard Bible Encyclopedia*.

is saying to us from God. Eli gives Hannah a blessing, and when she rises up, "*her face was no longer sad*" (1 Samuel 1:18). She has heard from God in her heart, and she is transformed—even though she knows the baby will come at a cost. Hannah's prayer and Eli's blessing bring great joy and peace. The Lord answers Hannah by redeeming her sense of emptiness and giving her the ability to rise up in newness of life. In due time, he will answer with a son. Samuel's life of service was the fruit of a mother's willingness to be transformed through prayer.

Reflect

Have you felt "barren" in some way? How has God met you there?

DAY

forty-seven

WHAT CAN WE LAY ASIDE?

READ RUTH 1:21–28

Many of us have read the Robert Frost poem, "The Road Not Taken." We know the story of how "two roads diverged in a yellow wood" and that the narrator took the one less traveled, which made "all the difference."[1] We wish every decision would end this way, with a sense of happiness and contentment that we have done the right thing. But in real life, decisions are hard, and we do not always know if we are making the right choices.

Hannah makes a difficult choice to keep her promise to God. She keeps Samuel at home until he is weaned, then honors her pledge to the Lord by taking him to Shiloh to serve under the priest. As part of her pledge, she reminds the priest that she was the woman he once accused: "*As you live, my lord, I am the woman who was standing here in your presence, praying to the LORD. For this child I prayed, and the LORD has granted me my petition that I made to him. Therefore I have lent him to the LORD. As long as he lives, he is lent to the LORD*" (1 Samuel 1:26–28). Hannah may have regretted her vow made in haste; she may have longed to keep her little son at home and raise him as her own. But her gratitude for Samuel's life and her promise to God overrides her own desires. Acknowledging the gifts we have received can help us overcome the things we must let go.

Loving sacrifice involves dying to things we once counted on. We

---

[1] Robert Frost, "The Road Not Taken," in *The Poetry of Robert* Frost, ed. Edward Connery Lathem (New York: Holt, Rinehart, and Winston, 1962).

may not be called to leave our child on the church steps—but we may be asked to lay down our pride, our need for recognition, our past regrets, or our dependence upon material things. We release our children when they grow up and are ready for their own lives; we release friends and neighbors when they move away. Hannah laid aside her own plans and ideas for raising a long-awaited son. God may ask you to let go of hopes and dependencies to find deeper satisfaction in him.

Reflect

Is there a past regret that you can lay down so you can follow God?

DAY forty-eight

HANNAH'S SONG

READ RUTH 2:1–10

After a long day of work as a chaplain, I don't usually feel like singing. After difficult visits with families struggling to find some hope, I find that all I can do is walk in the park and reflect on what I have seen and said. I am often reminded of how infrequently I give thanks to God for all I have, and I struggle to do this more often. I am impressed by Hannah's ability to sing in her situation. As I read Hannah's story more closely, however, I realize that her gratitude prompts her. She moves past fear into the risky arena of thankfulness.

Hannah's song is another kind of type scene. There are many embedded songs in the Old and New Testaments, and Mary's Magnificat is one. After Gabriel's prophecy, Mary responds by saying that she is only a humble servant and will do as God has said. Then she sings: *"My soul magnifies the Lord... for he who is mighty has done great things for me, and holy is his name"* (Luke 1:46–49). Other poems in the Bible include the Psalms of Ascent that pilgrims would sing along the way up to the temple in Jerusalem, Psalms 120–138. *"I was glad when they said unto me, 'Let us go to the house of the LORD! Our feet have been standing within your gates, O Jerusalem!'"* (Psalm 122:1–2). The song of Moses proclaims Israel's freedom when they crossed the Red Sea, *"The LORD is my strength and my song, and he has become my salvation"* (Exodus 15:2). The song of Deborah declares God's victory after Sisera has been defeated (Judges 5:2–31). The song of Simeon announces Simeon's gratitude to God when he sees the young Jesus: *"for my eyes have seen your salvation"* (Luke 2:30). In Hannah's song of gratitude, she proclaims that her *"heart exults in the LORD"* and her *"horn is exalted in the LORD,"* indicating that God has renewed her strength and transformed her heart (1 Samuel 2:1).

Hannah's song is both a blessing and a prophecy, proclaiming God as the one who gives hope to those who are ashamed. In Hannah's song, we see the first biblical reference to someone called the Lord's *"anointed,"* a king to come who would be Israel's hope (1 Samuel 2:10). God still gives us his hope and promises today. If singing doesn't work, you can find other ways to express thanks to God. You can write three things you are thankful for, call a friend, or pet your cat. Even simple acts of gratitude can remind you of God's kindness and fill your heart with joy.

Reflect

What are some simple ways that you can practice thankfulness?

DAY forty-nine

THE REST OF THE STORY

READ RUTH 2:11–21

For decades, radio personality Paul Harvey broadcasted human interest stories and unusual life vignettes. His daily closing segment was entitled "The Rest of the Story" and would complete an opener that had left listeners hanging. His closures always made us smile. This last segment of 2 Samuel is the rest of the story of Hannah's sorrow in longing for a child. She has left her cherished son at Shiloh to study with the priests. Her husband Elkanah returned home to Ramah without her, and Samuel stayed and *"ministered before the LORD under Eli the priest"* (1 Samuel 2:11 NIV). The rest of the story is about Hannah's years of supporting her son as he trains himself to one day lead Israel as a judge.

In contrast, Eli's sons have no respect for the Lord. Their thievery and deceit violated the Levitical law, which specified that the fat parts of an offering were to be burned by the priest as a *"pleasing aroma"* and not consumed (Leviticus 3). The priest's sons did not carry out the law of God. Meanwhile, Samuel listens and learns. Even as a boy, he ministers obediently and wears the priestly linen ephod. The text tells us that Hannah knits Samuel *"a little robe"* every year and takes it to Shiloh (1 Samuel 2:19). This robe was a soft, sleeveless gown worn under his scratchy priestly ephod. It would have been made as a labor of love. When Hannah delivers the garment, Eli blesses her and asks God to give her more children to replace the one she gave to God. The Lord answers, and Hannah's faithfulness to her promise and to her young son brings her a blessing that will, in turn, bless many.

Without his mother's support, Samuel might never have become a great leader. We all have opportunities to care for someone—a family member, a lonely neighbor, or a hurting friend. Think about who you might care for today. The person you help may be living out a godly purpose, and you can come alongside them with support and encouragement. Hannah didn't know what was coming for her son, just as we don't know what God has designed for others. But we know that when we love someone as God does, we can play a part in God's eternal plan. The rest of Hannah's story is that she carries out her part well.

Reflect

Read John 13:35: *"By this all people will know that you are my disciples, if you have love for one another."* To whom can you show loving care?

WEEK *eight*

LIVING

THE

RESTORED

LIFE

Honest prayer is a treasury of our highest thoughts about God.

what was coming for her son, just as we don't know what God has designed for others. But we know that when we love someone as God does, we can play a part in God's eternal plan. The rest of Hannah's story is that she carries out her part well.

Reflect

Read John 13:35: *"By this all people will know that you are my disciples, if you have love for one another."* To whom can you show loving care?

WEEK *eight*

LIVING THE RESTORED LIFE

> Honest prayer is a treasury of our highest thoughts about God.

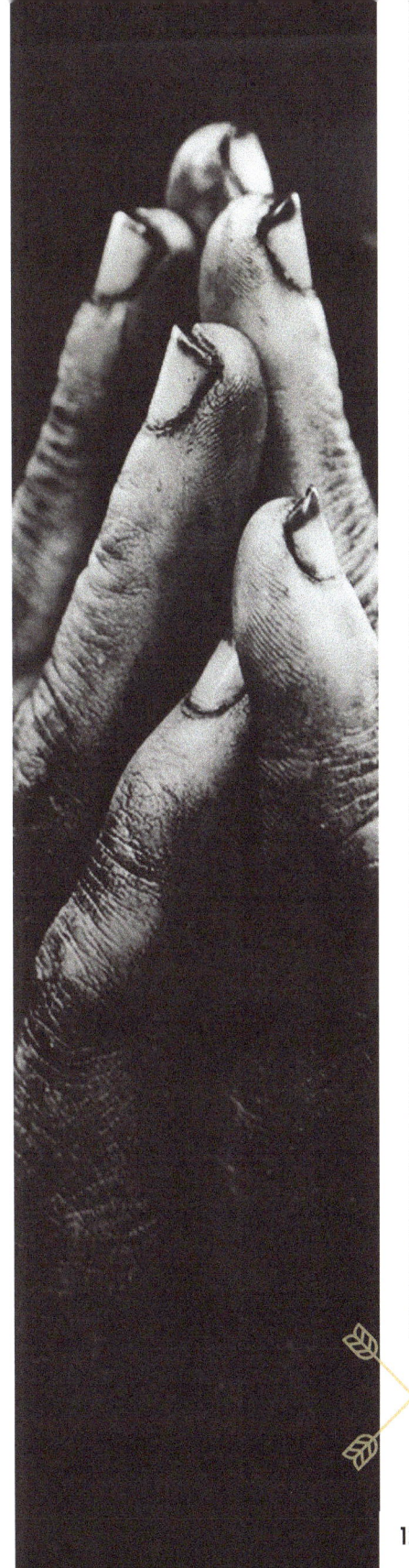

"When one rules justly over men, ruling in the fear of God, he dawns on them like the morning light."

2 SAMUEL 23:3–4

INTRODUCTION

King David ruled Israel between 1010 and 970 BC. His rise to kingship was unlikely, and his actions and choices had a supernatural quality that drew people to follow him. The Psalms of David are hymns and prayers that reveal a range of human emotions, from praise and thanksgiving to rage and sorrow. They are a lens into a great leader's honest prayer, and a treasury left for us to follow.

The character of David is as multi-dimensional as we are. David was a great king, an insightful poet, and a servant of God—but he was also a flawed sinner seeking the Lord. David's prayerful examples of honesty, lament, grief, repentance, and hope tell of a soul that is laid bare before the Lord. His joy and pain mirror our own experience, and through the window of his poetic writing, we have a picture of the true Messiah, Jesus Christ, who will come to heal all our grief and pain. As if completing the longing shown by Job, David's picture of the true Messiah is of an ultimate, eternal Kinsman-Redeemer.

In the devotionals for this final week, we will explore six themes from our study of the prayers of Job, Ruth, Hannah, and David. Viewed through the lens of a dying king's last words to his sons, 2 Samuel 23 encompasses many things—David's wisdom, his regrets, his lessons, and his hope for Israel. His prayer book gives us a window to his heart, connecting us to God and our desire for an abundant life of prayer.

DAY

PRAYER BUILDS OUR HOUSE

READ 1 KINGS 2:1–3; 2 SAMUEL 23:1

David's final words of prayer face the fact that life ends. One day, all of us will go "*the way of all the earth*" (1 Kings 2:2). Mercifully, Christians know that we are met by the hands of God. We may grieve as the world does, but not without hope. David is not despondent but speaks with authority and focus, even if conflicted about his coming death. He chooses to leave a legacy of strength for his house. His words in both 1 Kings and 2 Samuel, assumed to be written to his sons, show us his thoughts: "This is what I want you to remember; this is how to remain strong."

We, too, have conflicting feelings about our own death and the deaths of those we love. David gives us an example of how to take these fears back to God, leave a legacy of honoring him, and remain faithful. His first words to Solomon are, "*Be strong and show yourself a man, and keep the charge of the LORD your God, walking in his ways*" (1 Kings 2:2–3). Even in his pain and sorrow, David instructs his son about a life of prayer, a charge he received from God.

Consider the prayer, "*But I, through the abundance of your steadfast love, will enter your house. I will bow down toward your holy temple in the fear of you*" (Psalm 5:7–8). The temple of the Lord is where we find sanctuary, wisdom, blessing, and peace. We enter our own places of prayer to seek God for all his riches and grace, praising him and finding strength. God will meet us and lead us forward. A house for prayer can be a special place like a chapel, a quiet room, a prayer walk, or a mountain retreat—or it can be an everyday place like your closet, your car, or your kitchen table. If you are in Christ, you are God's temple and his Spirit dwells within you (1 Corinthians 3:16).

In the trial of Job and the journey of Ruth, strength of heart is a crucial key. Without a practice of prayer, we will have difficulty finding the strength we need to remain strong. David's last words are an oracle of sorts, given by a spiritually gifted soul. At the end of his life, he is called "*the man who was raised on high, the anointed of the God of Jacob, the sweet psalmist of Israel*" (2 Samuel 23:1).

Reflect

How can you use the prayers of David to build up your house of prayer?

DAY fifty-one

PRAYER HELPS US HEAR FROM GOD

READ 2 SAMUEL 23:2–3; 1 KINGS 2:3–4

I am in the habit of reading the chapter of the Psalms that matches the numbered day of the month. I sometimes add thirty to the day's number so that I can read the higher-numbered Psalms. I always pray for God to help me truly understand and teach me what I need to know. Today I read Psalm 20 in several translations. *"May [God] give you what your heart desires and fulfill your whole purpose"* (Psalm 20:4 CSB). I am reminded of my own search for purpose and calling and of the great desire in all of us to find meaning in life. Having a life focused on God at the center shows us the best way to serve and love. If you *"delight yourself in the LORD,"* he promises to meet you in your deepest longings and provide for your heart (Psalm 37:4).

David was a king whose life became purposeful over long years of loyalty to God. David's prayers laid the groundwork for his kingship, and throughout the Psalms, he describes the joy of ruling with justice and fear of God. When someone is a just ruler who humbly submits to God, he will be used by God as a tool for blessing others. David was God's instrument: *"The Spirit of the LORD speaks by me; his word is on my tongue"* (2 Samuel 23:2). This ability to listen well did not happen in a moment of glory; instead, David's life of honest prayer, supplication, lament, and praise forged a relationship that could discern God's voice.

Wisdom does not come from displaying a moment of piety or following a religious rule. It comes through steady obedience, love, and faith. When David rules justly, God begins to dawn on him *"like the morning light, like the sun shining forth on a cloudless morning, like rain that makes grass to sprout from the earth"* (2 Samuel 23:4). This same devotion undergirded Job's journey toward integrity, Ruth's choice to stay firm in her purpose, and Hannah's decision to find her voice and speak. David's example shows that if we seek God, we can hear him more clearly. We can seek God in various ways, as we make time to read God's Word, commit to pray for someone we love, or practice solitude and silence. David instructs his sons to rule justly, fear God, and lead others with grace (2 Samuel 23:3–4). When we pray honestly, we open the door for God to enter our hearts and speak.

Reflect

What do you need to hear from God through your prayers today?

DAY fifty-two

PRAYER HELPS US STAY CLOSE

READ 2 SAMUEL 23:5–6

One central theme that emerges from our study of Job, Ruth, and Hannah is that grief is a part of life. We all must cope with loss and grapple with sorrow, even when there are no clear answers and explanations. These stories of prayer reveal how God's love sustains us as we wrestle with life's difficulties. Samuel's record shows that David's life was full of disappointment and trials. But David comforted himself with God's promises: *"For does not my house stand so with God? For he has made with me an everlasting covenant, ordered in all things and secure"* (2 Samuel 23:5). David made mistakes and lost family, as we have. Still, he pursued a relationship with God.

Job, likewise, remained close to God as he struggled with the unexplained and heart-wrenching events of his life. In a desperate appeal, Job asked God: *"I know that you will bring me to death....Yet does not one in a heap of ruins stretch out his hand, and in his disaster cry for help?"* (Job 30:23–24). Job's prayer shows profound wisdom. Even though life hurts sometimes, I can still reach out to God, who loves me, and ask why. The Psalms provide examples for our questions. We are invited to speak plainly, cry out honestly, and ask for help.

Job's honesty and his persistent pounding at heaven's door invited an honest response from God. Ruth traveled far away from her family, culture, and friends. She must have had hard times and many questions. We don't have the true story of Ruth's inner thoughts, but her choices were likely conflicted as she became an alien in a strange land. Think of the millions of immigrants journeying from South America and Ukraine today; they don't know what awaits them, but they are following hope and a promise of safety. Hannah was a woman with a broken heart. She traveled to the altar of God throughout her desperate struggle to conceive. In her pain and embarrassment, God met her in her need. The Lord guided her to learn something she would not have otherwise: "Find me, Hannah. Find me through my Word and my Spirit, and then offer your heart and prayer back to me."

The Spirit of God reveals truth, no matter our circumstances. God honored Job's questions, Ruth's humility, and David's searching by providing wisdom. He will honor your questions as you seek him, too. God will continue to show you, "This is how you endure; this is how you love; this is what wholeness is; this is the shape of forgiveness, sorrow, beauty, and joy."[1]

Reflect

What are three things that closeness with God in prayer has offered you, even in loneliness or pain?

---

[1] Angela Gorrell, *The Gravity of Joy,* (Grand Rapids: Eerdmans, 2021), 121.

DAY

PRAYER IS A FORM OF SELF-ABANDONMENT

READ 2 SAMUEL 23:6–7

In a wonderful book entitled *Spirituality of the Psalms,* Walter Brueggemann explains the importance of David's Psalms of disorientation, when life is sometimes "savagely marked by incoherence, loss of balance, and asymmetry."[1] The church, Brueggemann claims, has often denied this and deceived people into thinking that they do not have to experience disorienting times. There is an unspoken assumption that abandoning composure would somehow let God down. But these stories testify to the opposite. Honest prayer *should* include opening our true selves to God. Only this "ceding of life over to its pioneer and perfecter," Brueggemann writes, can create the type of self-abandonment that admits along with the Westminster Confession of Faith: "The chief end of man is to glorify God and enjoy him forever."[2]

Each of the characters in our stories has left something behind—a family, an estate, a spiritual practice, or a beloved desire. Each person moved into a self-abandonment that received God's plan. Our characters' prayers changed throughout their narratives, just as David's prayers changed throughout his story. Although it would be some time until King David died, his prayer in 2 Samuel 23 is a heartfelt, final testimony to God's faithfulness. David left an extravagant kingship and power, but his life hidden in God was much more than all of this to him.

What is prayerful self-abandonment? There are many ways to pray,

---

1 Walter Brueggemann, *Spirituality of the Psalms* (Minneapolis: Fortress Press, 2002), 25–26.

2 Brueggemann, *Spirituality of the Psalms,* 57.

and different types of prayer speak to us uniquely. If we look for new ways to pray and walk with God, we can open our hearts. Brother Lawrence describes prayer as a "practice of the habitual presence of God, a familiarity with God's love and goodness."[3] One of Lawrence's prayer practices is the "breath prayer," a simple practice that expresses a heartfelt desire to be known by God. Linking yourself to the rhythm of your breathing, you breathe in and call on a biblical name or image of God, then breathe out a simple but God-given desire. For instance, breathe in, "Almighty Father," and breathe out, "please direct my path." The ancient Jesus Prayer is used worldwide: "Lord Jesus, Son of the Living God, have mercy on me, a sinner." This pattern echoes the prayer of the tax collector in Luke 18:13: *"God, be merciful to me, a sinner!"* Prayer begins with humble self-abandonment: *"For everyone who exalts himself will be humbled, but the one who humbles himself will be exalted"* (Luke 18:14).

Reflect

Ponder the line from the Westminster Confession of Faith. What would it mean for you to truly enjoy God today?

---

[3] "Brother Lawrence," in *Devotional Classics,* ed. Richard J. Foster (New York: HarperOne, 2005), 369–370.

DAY fifty-four

PRAYER ARMS US WITH JOY

READ 2 SAMUEL 23:7

I have a friend who recently faced a painful surgery to repair her spine. Throughout a season of faithful attendance at our church's evening prayer service, my friend, whose name translates as "healing agent," found the courage to move forward in trust. After her surgery, my friend said that she read the *Book of Common Prayer* daily because it helped her replace harmful thoughts with pure ones: "On dark days that I might struggle with doubt, I have to keep praying and read words of encouragement and hope, or I'll go under." Her words have been a constant reminder to me of how important our thoughts are for our healing. Many prayers in the *Book of Common Prayer* are a strong defense against discouragement. A favorite of mine reads: "O God of peace, who hast taught us that in returning and rest we will be saved, in quietness and confidence shall be our strength, we pray...that we may be still and know that thou art God."[1] Prayer arms us with hope.

In our study, we've seen the effects of prayer on four biblical characters. Each person sought deliverance and hope; their honest prayer was part of God's solution. Job hoped for an advocate, and God redeemed Job with new purpose. Ruth sought a near-kinsman to rescue her from widowhood, and in a field of ripe grain, Boaz appeared. Hannah prayed that she would be redeemed from shame, and she received and dedicated a son who became a wise judge over Israel. David contrasted God's protection of the righteous with his judgment for the wicked, for "*worthless men who are like thorns thrown*

---

1   *Book of Common Prayer, #59.*

away" (2 Samuel 23:6). God provided David with a humble heart. He armed himself physically with "*iron and the shaft of a spear,*" and in prayer, God armed David spiritually with courage and assurance (23:7).

For each hero, prayer became the solution. Seeking joy in God can heal a broken heart. Because joy comes from God, "there is no silence, imprisoned mind, or barren space that joy cannot break through."[2] Isaiah describes the work of the Spirit: *"to comfort all who mourn, to give them a beautiful headdress instead of ashes, the oil of gladness instead of mourning, the garment of praise instead of a faint spirit"* (Isaiah 61:2–3). God himself is our strength and shield (Psalm 18:1–2).

Reflect

How can you arm yourself today with joy?

---

[2] Angela Gorrell, *Gravity of Joy,* 128.

DAY

PRAYER REVEALS THAT JESUS LIVES

READ 2 SAMUEL 23

Psalms are examples of faith that help us understand how to engage our lives with God, and their fulfillment is found in the kingship of Jesus Christ. According to Walter Brueggemann, the Psalms are "genuinely dialogical literature that expresses...an entire gamut of speech to God, from profound praise to unspeakable anger and doubt."[1] David shows us how to pray. His treasury of poems and hymns beseech God and unlock the mystery of prayer; they are examples of how we know a Redeemer hears and responds.

The heartfelt prayers of Job, Ruth, and Hannah speak of a desperate need for rescue and hope. Job cries from the heart, claiming God as salvation: *"For I know that my Redeemer lives, and at the last he will stand upon the earth"* (Job 19:25). Ruth confesses her great need for rescue: *"I am Ruth, your servant. Spread your wings over your servant, for you are a redeemer"* (Ruth 3:9). Hannah admits to the priest, *"I am a woman troubled in spirit...pouring out my soul before the LORD"* (1 Samuel 1:15). As we have seen, God answers their prayers by teaching them to pray and seek him.

Throughout the entire treasury of the Psalms, David confesses his deep need for a savior. He holds nothing back. What David writes is "scandalous, but states what must be said about the human situation. It is said directly to Yahweh, Lord of human experience and partner in it all."[2] In 2 Samuel 23, David regrets many things but appeals to God for rescue

---

1   Brueggemann, *Spirituality of the Psalms,* 1–2.
2   Brueggemann, *Spirituality of the Psalms,* 30.

and forgiveness. Without knowing the reality of what would come to pass in Jesus, David promises his sons that God will provide an eternal Advocate one day. We know this Son of God as the source of forgiveness, restoration, and peace. He is the Redeemer who protected Job and the eternal Kinsman who rescued Ruth. The Psalms are a window into David's relationship with God, a lifelong prayer book of the king, and a handbook to encourage our trust in the Messiah.

Reflect

How does knowing that your Redeemer lives give you hope in what you face today?

DAY fifty-six

BIRTH, DEATH, REBIRTH, AND RESURRECTION

REVIEW OF HONEST PRAYER

Julian of Norwich was a Benedictine nun who lived between 1343–1413 and became one of the most popular English mystics. For a time, she lived in a small cave attached to the church, to be near people who came for healing and solace. Her book, *Revelations of Divine Love*, describes the link between Christ's passion and resurrection. Her writing focuses on the goodness and love of God that is a light for anyone who calls on his name. "Joy is the keynote of emotions in her life," says Richard Foster in his introduction to her story. Foster explains that Julian trusted in the goodness of God's threefold revelation, promising us, "All shall be well, and all manner of things shall be well." In one memoir entitled "The Highest Form of Prayer," Julian writes that we pray to know God's passion—which comes from his complete goodness and ultimate love. "We pray for strength from the Cross and the help of the saints—all from the goodness of God that gives life to our souls."[1]

The metaphor of birth, death, and rebirth is a theme in our study of Honest Prayer. Job, Ruth, Hannah, and David each experienced a death—death of a family and way of life, death of a dream and a homeland, a loss of hope for motherhood, and the death of an ideal reign. By God's grace, these characters found the deep renewal that gives them the strength to love well, embrace their destiny, and leave a legacy of hope. Death leads to rebirth and renewal.

---

1 "Julian of Norwich: The Highest Form of Prayer," in *Devotional Classics*, ed. Richard J. Foster, 73.

When we look at the seasons, the moon, the tide, and all nature, we find confirmation of the beauty of life when it begins to renew. When we experience God in prayer, answering us and coming to us in new, unanticipated ways, we are made aware of his abiding presence—a presence that always offers new life.

An anonymous author composed a document that describes a resurrected life blessed by contemplation and worship. This advice on the spiritual life is published as *The Cloud of Unknowing: Where only Love Can Go* and describes God as "higher than our minds and our best efforts at language."[2] I will close with an excerpt from one of the prayers:

"It is time for you to look ahead and forget what is behind you, time to pay attention to what you still need and not what you had. And what is ahead, if you are to make spiritual progress, is a life lived in desire, a desire that will always, through God's power and your consent, be at work in your soul."[3]

---

[2] *The Cloud of Unknowing: Where only Love Can Go,* ed. John Kirvan (Notre Dame, IN: Ave Maria Press, 2009), 1.

[3] *The Cloud of Unknowing,* 17.

STUDY
guide

WEEK One

JOB 1–14

THE MYSTERY OF GOD'S SOVEREIGNTY

KEY VERSE:

God is *"wise in heart and mighty in strength—who has hardened himself against him, and succeeded?"* (Job 9:4).

OPENING PRAYER:

Lord God, you are all-powerful and above all things that we could ask or imagine. Renew our hearts today as we study what your word says about honest prayer. Open our hearts to learn from the story of Job.

GUIDING QUESTION:

What does it look like to wrestle with God as we experience life's disappointments?

SESSION INTRODUCTION:

Life is full of joy, celebration, pain, and disappointment. Although God is not always the author of our struggles, he is the presence behind the outcomes and encourages us to seek him in our lives. One way to work through unexpected disappointment is to turn to God in honest prayer. To understand this process, however, we must first see who God is and trust him to provide answers. Job is a character who struggled with these issues and came to know God as Redeemer, sovereign Creator, and loving Provider. Job's journey begins with prayer.

Honest prayer reflects our trust in God. We begin with a willingness to be authentic with our open and unfiltered thoughts. No matter what takes place in our lives, Scripture invites us to come before a holy God, reveal our deepest needs, confess our sins, and ask for help. Job remains honest with God, even though he wrestles with disappointment and pain. As we approach God with trust, we draw close to the source of our deepest joy.

SECTION 1

GATHER: ACKNOWLEDGING OUR NEED

1. Have you considered the book of Job to be a story about honest prayer?

2. When have you experienced a "spiritual wilderness"? How did you discover that God was meeting you there?

WATCH THE VIDEO >> https://biblestudymedia.com/honestprayer.

VIDEO NOTES:

LIVING A RIGHTEOUS LIFE

- Understanding God's sovereign mystery
- Understanding God's righteousness
- Understanding disappointment

SECTION 2

GROW: WRESTLING WITH GOD'S PROVIDENCE

3. Do you struggle with understanding why God allowed Satan to tempt Job? Look at Job 1:8. What do God's descriptions prove?

4. What does Job's wife suggest after Satan strikes him a second time (2:9)? Why does he not accept this cruel comment?

5. What do you think about Job lamenting the day of his birth in 3:11? Where do you see this same attitude today?

6. Job's friend Eliphaz claims that innocent people will prosper (chapter 5). Do you believe his logic today?

SECTION 3

GO: EMBRACING OUR REDEMPTION

7. Job asks God, *"Why do you not pardon my transgression?"* and looks for an arbiter to defend him (7:21). Who has acted in the role of arbiter for you, and how did that make you feel?

8. Job confesses that God is the author of wisdom, counsel, and understanding (12:13). He pledges, *"Though he slay me, I will hope in him"* (13:15). How can we still hope in God when things fall apart?

CLOSING PRAYER:

"Almighty and everlasting God, you made the universe with all its marvelous order, its atoms, worlds, and galaxies, and the infinite complexity of living creatures: Grant that, as we probe the mysteries of your creation, we may come to know you more truly, and more surely fulfill our role in your eternal purpose; in the name of Jesus Christ our Lord" (Book of Common Prayer, Prayers and Thanksgivings, 40).

WEEK *Two*

JOB 15–30

LISTENING TO THE COUNSEL OF FRIENDS

KEY VERSE:

"I know that my Redeemer lives, and at the last he will stand upon the earth" (Job 19:25).

OPENING PRAYER:

"My God, I want to give myself to you. Give me this courage. My spirit within me sighs after you. Strengthen my will. If I don't have the strength to give You everything, then draw me by the sweetness of Your love and your guidance. Lord, who do I belong to, if not to You?"[1]

GUIDING QUESTION:

Where do you turn for help or rescue when life seems unfair?

SESSION INTRODUCTION:

Sometimes we want to flee when things get hard. We fear that our perplexing questions will never be answered and that our worries about life and death will never be explained. Many of us wonder why wicked people succeed, and in despair, we avoid asking God our deeper questions. Job's predicament draws the attention of others, and Job is almost forced to seek out their advice. His counselors are well-meaning friends, but they do not understand his desperate cry of the heart. In his friends' eyes, there is no justice in suffering. Each friend develops a unique case for why Job is tormented—and all their reasoning is based on man's responsibility. As we study Job, we will learn that bearing this responsibility for all life's events is not what God designed.

Life often seems unfair. Job seeks God through his spiritual fog and does not depend on advice from his friends. He wrestles with questions but does not give up on the God he knows from experience. He concludes that God knows the path to wisdom, and God will lead him by faith.

---

[1] François Fénelon, *The Complete Fenelon*, trans. and ed. Robert J. Edmonson and Hal M. Helms (Brewster, MA: Paraclete Press, 2008), 128.

SECTION 1

GATHER: ACKNOWLEDGING OUR NEED

Job's friend Eliphaz challenges him by asking, "*What is man, that he can be pure?*" (15:14). When have you had similar unhelpful advice from a friend?

Job turns to God with his questions: "*Even now, behold, my witness is in heaven, and he who testifies for me is on high!*" (16:19). When you face struggles, where do you turn—to others or to God in prayer?

WATCH THE VIDEO >> https://biblestudymedia.com/honestprayer.

VIDEO NOTES:

THE WELL-MEANING COUNSEL OF FRIENDS

- Job as a story of Hebrew exile and return
- Job as a recipient of advice from friends
- Job as an example of humility and holiness in suffering

SECTION 2

GROW: WRESTLING WITH GOD'S PROVIDENCE

Zophar says, "*Agree with God, and be at peace, so good will come to you*" (22:21). Job's friends judge him as a bad person since he is not receiving good things. In your experience, does Zophar's reasoning hold true?

Job struggles to find an arbiter: "*Oh, that I knew where I might find him...then I would lay my case before him and fill my mouth with arguments!*" (23:3–4). Do you ever feel like God is not listening? What do you do at such times? Job's friend Bildad claims, "*How then can man be in the right before God? How can he who is born of woman be pure?*" (25:4). Is being "right" before God based on what is done or left undone?

The Wisdom Hymn states: "*God understands the way, and he knows its place. For he looks to the ends of the earth and sees everything under the heavens*" (Job 28:23–24). What does this help you see?

SECTION 3

GO: EMBRACING OUR REDEMPTION

How do we continue to walk with God when things are hard? Where do you look for wisdom when life doesn't turn out as you hoped?

"*I put on righteousness, and it clothed me,*" Job concludes (29:14). What is God's view of righteousness? See Romans 5:1–5.

CLOSING PRAYER:

"*I have labored in vain; I have spent my strength for nothing and vanity; yet surely my right is with the LORD, and my recompense with my God.*" (Isaiah 49:4). Help us, Lord, as we seek your ways to know that we are safe within your love. Help us seek you with all our hearts and believe what you have said. In Christ Jesus, who made a way for us to know you, Amen.

WEEK Three

JOB 31-38

SEEKING GOD AS MEDIATOR

KEY VERSE:

"If there be for him an angel, a mediator…he will declare to man what is right" (Job 33:23).

OPENING PRAYER:

Lord God, open our hearts to hear you through your Word. Let this story of Job teach us about your sovereignty and our smallness in the face of your glory. Help us see ourselves more clearly as we learn to look to you.

GUIDING QUESTION:

How do we wait for God's answers and direction when he seems far away?

SESSION INTRODUCTION:

Many times in life, we just don't know what to do. We are frustrated with our efforts to set things right, and we wonder why God doesn't seem to respond to our prayers. We need an intercessor to take our hopes and pleas to heaven—and translate God's response, so we can choose what is right. We need a mediator between our sinful selves and a perfect, holy God.

Mediators were an essential part of the world of the Bible. In the ancient Near East, mediators represented the poor in disputes and misunderstandings. Esther, for example, was an ideal mediator because she belonged both to the Jews and the Persian king. In the New Testament, the centurion sent Jewish elders as mediators to ask Jesus to heal a beloved servant (Luke 7:1–5). Mediators were skilled speakers who would "advocate upward" in ancient collective societies for people who could not advocate for themselves.

Job has a complaint against God, but he and God are not equals. There is a "massive power gap between Job and God."[1] Job cannot say enough to

---

1   E. Randolph Richards and Richard James, *Misreading Scripture with Individualist Eyes* (Downers Grove, IL: IVP Academic, 2020), 112.

prove his innocence, and he continues to lament the lack of justice. Job's friends have encouraged him to accept his lot, and none of them can make things right. If only there were "*an arbiter between us,*" Job prays, "*who might lay his hand on us both...Then I would speak without fear of him, for I am not so in myself.*" (9:33, 35).

SECTION 1

GATHER: ACKNOWLEDGING OUR NEED

Job's story is not easy to understand. Is there a time you wanted to give up, but God came into your story in a loving way?

Job lamented, "*My dignity is driven away as by the wind, my safety vanishes like a cloud*" (30:15 NIV). What trial have you asked God to remove?

WATCH THE VIDEO >> https://biblestudymedia.com/honestprayer.

VIDEO NOTES:

WHAT IS A MEDIATOR AND WHY DO WE NEED ONE?

- Mediator's history in the Hebrew sacrificial system
- Mediator as the Good Shepherd
- Mediator as the restorer of righteousness

SECTION 2

GROW: WRESTLING WITH GOD'S PROVIDENCE

What do you learn about different ways of hearing from God in Job 33:12–16?

Job claims, "*Although I am guiltless, his arrow inflicts an incurable wound*" (34:6 NIV). Are Job's wounds a result of his guilt?

Do you agree with Elihu that "*God is mighty...He does not keep the wicked alive, but gives the afflicted their right*" (36:5–6). How is this an overly simplistic explanation for God's action in the world?

SECTION 3

GO: EMBRACING OUR REDEMPTION

God speaks in Job 38. What words describing God's authority give you comfort and security?

Job 36:22–23 says, *"God is exalted in his power; who is a teacher like him?"* What have you learned from God in times of pain?

CLOSING PRAYER:

"Almighty God, ruler of all things in heaven and earth, hear our prayers for the church family. Strengthen the faithful, arouse the careless, and restore the penitent. Grant us all things necessary for our common life and bring us all to be of one heart and mind within your holy Church, through Jesus Christ our Lord" (Book of Common Prayer, Prayers and Thanksgivings, Prayers for the Church, 11).

WEEK Four

JOB 39–42

ARRIVING AT WISDOM

KEY VERSE:

"*I know that you can do all things, and that no purpose of yours can be thwarted*" (Job 42:2).

OPENING PRAYER:

"Oh God and Father of all, whom the whole heavens adore: Let the whole earth worship you, all nations obey you, all tongues confess and bless you, and men and women everywhere love you and serve you in peace, through Jesus Christ our Lord" (Book of Common Prayer, Evening Prayer, Rite II).

GUIDING QUESTION:

What can we learn about God's greater purposes through our suffering?

SESSION INTRODUCTION:

Job is a book of Wisdom Literature, written in part to explain how to find wisdom in times of need. For centuries, man has wondered: how can a benevolent God allow suffering? Holy men have tried to answer this difficult question. Jewish holy books were divided into three main divisions: the Law, the Prophets, and the Writings. The Psalms and other types of wisdom materials such as Job, Proverbs, and Ecclesiastes were read for instruction and encouragement. Wisdom Literature developed over time as the sages sought answers to troubling questions. These learned men had excellent knowledge of the world, insight into human relationships, and wise counsel about success and failure. While priests focused on moral and religious concerns, sages focused on the practical aspects of life and ambiguities in our human experience.

The author of the book of Job was likely an Israelite sage who wanted his story to be told. He wrote to godly sufferers who, like Job, were experiencing a crisis of faith. The book's tone shows that he may have known Job and had great empathy for his pain. Having listened to priests and theologians of the day, the author communicated their perspectives. They speak as Job's friends, but they offer only *"miserable comfort"* (16:2). The book of Job suggests that when people suffer, our human minds struggle to understand. In the end, the author leads us to trust that suffering is part of our humanity. Job shows us what true, tested godliness and humility can be.

SECTION 1

GATHER: ACKNOWLEDGING OUR NEED

Acknowledging God's wisdom brings Job peace. How has finding true wisdom offered peace to you?

We cannot explain all that takes place in life but can choose to remain faithful. Is it hard to let go of needing to have all the answers?

WATCH THE VIDEO >> https://biblestudymedia.com/honestprayer.

VIDEO NOTES:

SEEING GOD'S WISDOM

- God addresses our needs.
- God describes himself in metaphors and parables.
- God has no equal.

SECTION 2

GROW: WRESTLING WITH GOD'S PROVIDENCE

God states that he can *"take [Behemoth] by the eyes, or pierce his nose with a snare"* (Job 40:24). Given this image, do you believe God can overcome issues that trouble you?

Job finally stops wrestling. Examine the steps of Job's honest prayer in 42:1–6. What gives you a sense of security from this passage?

Name the three blessings God uses to restore Job. Have you experienced these same blessings?

SECTION 3

GO: EMBRACING OUR REDEMPTION

God paints himself as the source of all wisdom. What words convey this truth?

What have you learned about honest prayer from studying Job? What spiritual truth can you apply?

CLOSING PRAYER:

Father God, thank you for all we can learn from Job. Let our hearts be turned toward you and your faithful abundance; let us repent when you call us to our knees; let us see you for who you really are—the great I AM who is above all things. In Jesus's name, Amen.

WEEK Five

RUTH 1–2

GOD'S PROVIDENCE PROVIDES HOPE

KEY VERSE:

"And she said, 'See, your sister-in-law has gone back to her people and to her gods; return after your sister-in-law.' But Ruth said, 'Do not urge me to leave you or to return from following you. For where you go I will go, and where you lodge I will lodge. Your people shall be my people, and your God my God'" (Ruth 1:15–16).

OPENING READING:

"True prayer is simply another name for the love of God. Its excellence does not consist in the multitude of our words, for our Father knows what we need before we ask him. True prayer is prayer of the heart, and the heart prays only for what it desires. To pray, then, is to desire or long for, but to desire what God would have us desire. Those who ask, but not from the bottom of their hearts, are mistaken in thinking that they are praying."[1]

GUIDING QUESTION:

How do we trust God's providence in our lives when we are tempted to lose hope?

SESSION INTRODUCTION:

    The book of Ruth tells the story of God's redeeming love in a world of uncertainty, inequality, and disappointment. Ruth is not so different from you or me. She left a previous life and moved to a new city. She wrestled with death, disappointment, and distance from her family. Though not her original plan, Ruth chose to live and travel with her extended family. It is in this place of trust, however, where Ruth discovers God's blessing. Sometimes we must walk through wilderness times alone to see God more clearly and hear him speak to our hearts.

    Like Ruth, God may be leading you on a journey that will require your trust and courage. As Ruth and Naomi walk through a desert of their grief, they are given new identities that replace their former assumptions. Sometimes it takes a journey alone to find what we are made of, what we can endure, and

---

1   François Fénelon, *The Complete Fenelon*, 85.

what we must be willing to let go. In her bitterness, Naomi almost missed the blessings God had for her. In a moment of indecision, Ruth almost turned the other way. We may miss the loving hand of God if we do not seek his provision and care.

When we walk with God, his Word promises that we will gain more than we release (Mark 10:28–30). Our journey of faith will take a lifetime. In this story, Naomi, Ruth, and Boaz each choose a new and unexpected life. Their choices reveal their faith and courage, and the new beginnings bless many for generations to come.

SECTION 1

GATHER: ACKNOWLEDGING OUR NEED

Naomi experienced famine, a cross-country move, and the death of her sons. How did her loneliness draw her to God? Can you identify with her?

Read Naomi's first prayer found in 1:8. What was her cost to return home? Describe a time when you had to trust God to help you let go.

WATCH THE VIDEO >> https://biblestudymedia.com/honestprayer.

VIDEO NOTES:

WHAT WAS THE TIME OF THE JUDGES?

- Understanding the importance of setting: "*In those days there was no king in Israel. Everyone did what was right in his own eyes*" (Judges 21:25).
- Understanding collective cultures, names, clans
- Recognizing the value of divine appointments

SECTION 2

GROW: WRESTLING WITH GOD'S PROVIDENCE

Boaz marries a woman outside of his race. Jesus extends his hand to Samaritans and outcasts. How can you connect with people who are not part of your religious or cultural crowd?

What type of prayer helps Naomi leave her bitterness behind? How has prayer helped you forgive someone?

What is the meaning behind Boaz inviting Ruth to "*eat some bread and dip your morsel in the wine*" (Ruth 2:14)? What does this image bring to mind?

Ruth does not wrestle with God but instead trusts Yahweh with her future. What holds you back from trusting God?

SECTION 3

GO: EMBRACING OUR REDEMPTION

Ruth faced an important test when she promised, "*Where you go I will go*" (Ruth 1:16). Who was Ruth really following? How is your loyalty to God tested?

Does knowing God is with you as Redeemer change how you respond to trying circumstances?

CLOSING PRAYER:

"Heavenly Father, we thank you for making the earth fruitful, so that it might produce what is needed for life; Bless those who work in the fields; give us seasonable weather; and grant that we may all share the fruits of the earth, rejoicing in your goodness, through Jesus Christ our Lord" (Book of Common Prayer, Prayers and Thanksgivings, 29).

GOING DEEPER:

How can your suffering help to produce perseverance, character, and hope, as Paul suggests in Romans 5:3–5?

What actions of God's providence have helped you make sense of your own journey?

WEEK Six

RUTH 3-4

IN ALL THINGS, GOD IS WORKING FOR OUR GOOD

KEY VERSE:

"*Boaz took Ruth, and she became his wife. . . and the LORD gave her conception, and she bore a son. Then the women said to Naomi, 'Blessed be the LORD, who has not left you this day without a redeemer, and may his name be renowned in Israel! He shall be to you a restorer of life and a nourisher of your old age'*" (Ruth 4:13–15).

OPENING PRAYER:

Holy God, help us rest in you. Help us remember that you are working behind the scenes of our lives. Allow us to trust your promise that "*the Spirit intercedes for the saints according to the will of God. And we know that for those who love God all things work together for good*" (Romans 8:27–28).

GUIDING QUESTION:

Can we trust God to bring good out of seemingly tragic events?

SESSION INTRODUCTION:

  This week introduces some old-world cultural terms like kinsman-redeemer, the rule of the Levir, the Go'El, and the threshing floor. We will see how these terms beautifully point to a larger design of God that was ultimately fulfilled in Christ. Ruth begins as a marginalized person dependent on an extended family who will graft her into the family of God. She depends on a kinsman-redeemer to marry her, but as she yields to the family of Yahweh, her role expands, and her lineage leads to Israel's greatest king. Boaz invites God's blessing upon Ruth: "*A full reward be given you by the LORD, the God of Israel, under whose wings you have come to take refuge*" (Ruth 2:12). Boaz's prayer shows his acceptance of his prescribed role as a Levirate male, charged with protection, refuge, rescue, and care. He forecasts the larger role that Jesus will play as the Savior who takes the church as his bride. Ruth's request, "*Spread your cloak over me*" (Ruth 3:9 CSB), becomes an invitation for Boaz to act as a servant-leader who rescues her, taking on Ruth, her mother-in-law, and any property the family might have. The Lord builds the bridge between their families for his greater purpose, and he will do the same for us.
  In our lives and in the story of Ruth, only God brings abundance out of emptiness and loss. The threshing floor of a barn, not unlike the floor

under a manger, is where the plot turns from despair to grace. While Boaz is separating the wheat from the chaff, tossing the grain into the sky, God is setting Ruth apart for himself to bear his family line. Metaphors and imagery abound in this well-crafted ancient story, but Ruth's simple story is also our own. When we are open to God's plan, he will use us to bring his joy to others and make us part of his kingdom.

SECTION 1

GATHER: ACKNOWLEDGING OUR NEED

Ruth boldly obeys Naomi's instruction to visit the family redeemer. Have you ever approached someone you did not know out of obedience to God?

Do you feel you can approach Jesus in times of need? What might you ask?

WATCH THE VIDEO >> https://biblestudymedia.com/honestprayer.

VIDEO NOTES:

GOD PROVIDES FOR OUR RESCUE AND SECURITY

- Understanding kinship and *hesed*
- Appreciating the prophetic value of levirate marriage
- Seeing the threshing floor as a metaphor for atonement

SECTION 2

GROW: WRESTLING WITH GOD'S PROVIDENCE

Naomi prays for Ruth to find favor with Boaz, and God provides. How has God provided for you in a time of need?

Boaz admits that he is a redeemer who will take Ruth under his wing. Who has God provided to show love to you during a difficult time?

The elders rejoice at Ruth's betrothal like a "*cloud of witnesses*" (Hebrews 12:11). What role have friends and relatives played in your spiritual growth?

Ruth's son Obed becomes an ancestor of King David. Read Ephesians 1:3–14. What spiritual blessings do we receive from our inheritance as Christians?

SECTION 3

GO: EMBRACING OUR REDEMPTION

God brings good out of Ruth and Naomi's lonely situation, and both are redeemed. What inspires you about this part of Ruth's story?

At the end of the book, Naomi experiences emotional and spiritual healing. What part of your soul might need healing from the Lord?

CLOSING PRAYER:

"May God the Father bless you, God the Son heal you, and God the Spirit give you strength. May the Holy Trinity guard your body, save your soul, and bring you safely to his heavenly country where he lives and reigns forever" (Book of Common Prayer, Prayers for the Sick, 460).

WEEK Seven

1 SAMUEL 1–2:21

THE DIFFICULT PROCESS OF ASKING GOD

KEY VERSE:

"'As you live, my lord, I am the woman who was standing here in your presence, praying to the LORD. For this child I prayed, and the LORD has granted me my petition that I made to him. Therefore I have lent him to the LORD. As long as he lives, he is lent to the LORD.' And he worshiped the LORD there" (1 Samuel 1:26–28).

OPENING PRAYER:

Father God, where we are weak, you are strong. Please give us the courage to tell you how we feel and ask for what we need, even when life seems unmanageable. Help us, like Hannah, to take our desires to you and remember that no secrets are hidden from you. Help us trust that you hear us and will answer our prayer in your love. In Jesus's name, Amen.

GUIDING QUESTION:

Do you wrestle with the difficulty of asking God for something you deeply long for?

SESSION INTRODUCTION:

   The story of Hannah and her heartfelt prayer is a story of a woman seeking a child. But more than that, it is the story of a woman seeking a voice, a name, and a place in God's plan. Hannah is bold, honest, and brave. The elements of her story—her need, bravery, and hope—are examples for us. Hannah inspires us to pour out our hearts before the Lord and look for his answers. Often, God's answers are more about God and his love for us than about our wants and desires, and experience with God allows us to realize this. Hannah's bold prayer encourages us not to be afraid to admit our fears but to come to God in trust and openness.
   Hannah longed for a child and a role in God's work. We all hope for many things that remain unfulfilled, and over the course of a life, we must lay aside dreams and set aside opportunities. But while we wait and sacrifice, God encourages us to find satisfaction in him. Hannah's prayer pours out her gratitude to God because he has heard her request. We experience this

same joy when we hear from God or see what he has done in surprising new ways. Hannah conceived a child, but God also renewed Hannah's worth in his image. God restores her strength, gives her purpose, and builds her resolve. When we lift our hands in honest prayer, we will find the same.

SECTION 1

GATHER: ACKNOWLEDGING OUR NEED

Are there any experiences that have caused you to feel disappointed or abandoned by God?

Re-read 1 Samuel 1:2–10. What parts of God's character can you rely on as you wait to understand his plan?

WATCH THE VIDEO >> https://biblestudymedia.com/honestprayer.

VIDEO NOTES:

THE PRIESTLY SACRIFICE AND GOD'S PRESENCE

- Who is the author?
- What is a type scene?
- What is the significance of Hannah's prayer?

SECTION 2

GROW: WRESTLING WITH GOD'S PROVIDENCE

Read 1 Samuel 1.
Hannah is taunted by Peninnah. Has anyone ever mocked you for your faith?

Do you pray with trust and honesty? Using Hannah's prayer in faith as a guide, what would you ask for today?

Jesus tells us to pray with an attitude that will "*ask, seek and knock*" (Matthew 7:7). Do you feel assured that God hears when you ask and knock at the door?

Hannah draws on God's grace to stand up to accusations. Can you depend on God's grace in life?

SECTION 3

GO: EMBRACING OUR REDEMPTION

Eli blesses Hannah and asks for God's peace (1 Samuel 1:17). She, in turn, blesses Eli. What blessing can you pray over someone you love?

Hannah's prayer was a response to God's promised redemption. What promise could you make to God in response to his remembering you?

CLOSING PRAYER:

"*In You, O LORD, do I take refuge; Let me never be put to shame! In your righteousness deliver me and rescue me; incline your ear to me, and save me!*" (Psalm 71:1–2).

GOING DEEPER:

Read 1 Samuel 2:1–10.

What verses in Hannah's emotional prayer remind you of Job's story? What do you admire most about Hannah's character?

WEEK Eight

2 SAMUEL 22–23:1–7

LIVING THE RESTORED LIFE

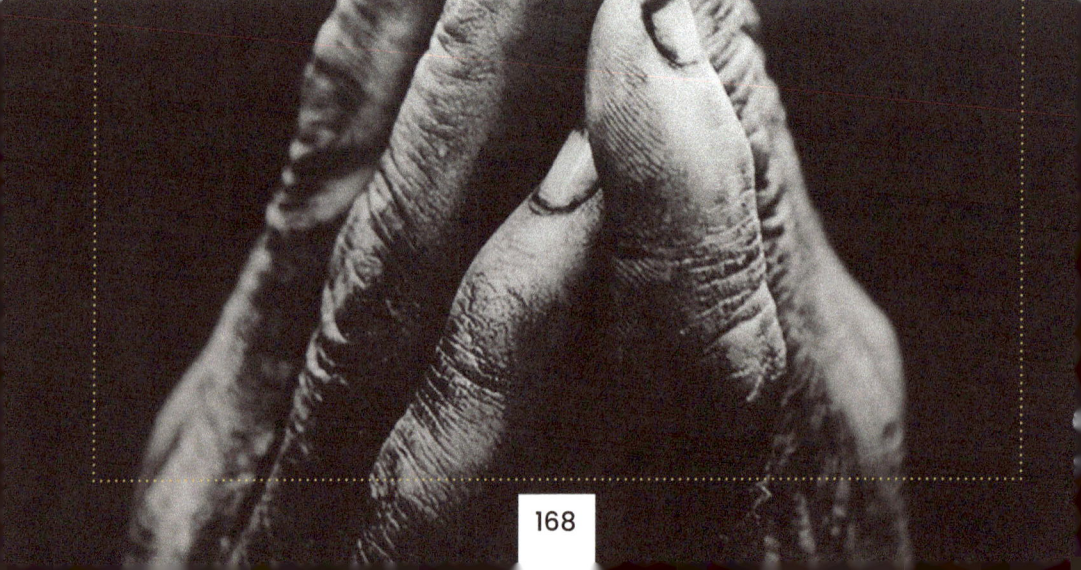

KEY VERSE:

"*The Rock of Israel has said to me: When one rules justly over men, ruling in the fear of God, he dawns on them like the morning light, like the sun shining forth on a cloudless morning, like rain that makes grass to sprout from the earth*" (2 Samuel 23:3–4).

OPENING READING:

"Lift up your heart continually to God. He will purify, enlighten, and direct it. Try to be able to say with the holy King David, 'I have set the LORD always before me,' and again, 'Whom have I in heaven but you? And earth has nothing I desire besides you…God is the strength of my heart and my portion forever.' You must be regular with such spiritual reading…even a few words studied in this way are true manna to the soul. You may forget the actual words, but they are taking root all the time secretly, and your soul will feed upon them and be strengthened."[1]

GUIDING QUESTION:

How does a broken but restored life produce a legacy of godly wisdom?

SESSION INTRODUCTION:

What would happen if we realized that our dreams for worldly success are not God's highest purpose for us? We may think that God is leading us to a life of noble vocation, moral decisions, or social respect—but what if God is interested instead in the *process* part of our lives, the part that wades through the mud? What if reaching a particular applauded end is not God's aim? From the characters in our study of honest prayer, we can conclude that God's purpose for us is to depend on him and his power in our lives. Rather than working toward our fame and success, God may be building our godliness. His greatest desire may be that we recognize his work and give him glory in

---

1 François Fénelon, *The Complete Fenelon,* 70.

all that we do. Trusting God is the most God-glorifying posture we can assume throughout our lives.

In the prayer known as "David's Last Words," King David leaves a legacy, even in his broken confession. Having waded through victories, guilt, trauma, and challenge, David chooses to remain a "*man after God's own heart*" (1 Samuel 13:14). The Psalms are our greatest examples of honest prayer. David struggles (as we do) with human sin, false idols, and temptation—yet he climbs back to God in prayer, supplication, and thanksgiving. Like Hannah, David pours out his heart in prayer; like Job, David wrestles with God; and, like Ruth, David acknowledges God's provision in his time of need. David's honesty about his emotions gives us the freedom to unveil our own desires. David climbs under God's wing and rests in God's steadfast love.

SECTION 1

GATHER: ACKNOWLEDGING OUR NEED

David's "Song of Praise" in 2 Samuel 22 contains verses from many Psalms. How do these verses speak to you?

Notice 2 Samuel 22:32–33. What parallels do you see between these statements and the prayers of Job and Hannah?

WATCH THE VIDEO >> https://biblestudymedia.com/honestprayer.

VIDEO NOTES:

THE HIGHS AND LOWS OF DAVID'S REIGN

- Understanding David's address
- Understanding David's anointing
- Understanding David's rule in the fear of God

SECTION 2

GROW: WRESTLING WITH GOD'S PROVIDENCE

Read Psalm 51.

According to Psalm 51, what was David's greatest desire and deepest struggle? What do you want from a life with God?

In Psalm 51, David looks to God to restore his broken heart. Have you experienced a broken heart, and how does this Psalm help you?

Inspired as a shepherd, David was anointed by Samuel and became the king and hero of Israel. Do you believe God is calling you to a heroic story?

How did David learn to *"rule justly over men, ruling in the fear of God"* (23:4)? What faith lessons has God used to teach you about righteous living?

SECTION 3

GO: EMBRACING OUR REDEMPTION

Psalm 51:5–7 summarizes David's regret and God's restoration. What are some things you regret in life? How has God redeemed one of your past mistakes?

David navigated many thorns in his life (Psalm 23:6). How has God helped you learn to cast aside thorns as you walk closer with him?

CLOSING PRAYER:

"Accept, O Lord, our thanks and praise for all you have done for us. We thank you for the splendor of all creation…. We thank you also for disappointments and failures that lead us to acknowledge our dependence on you alone. Above all, we thank you for your son, Jesus Christ, for the truth of his Word and the example of his life" (Book of Common Prayer, General Thanksgiving).

GOING DEEPER:

How does David's imperfect life inspire you to be more open with God?

What have you learned from David's last words about your own prayer life?

APPENDICES

FREQUENTLY ASKED *questions*

What do we do on the first night of our group?

Have a party! A "get to know you" coffee, dinner, or dessert is a great way to launch a new study. You may want to review the Small Group Covenant (page 179) and share the names of a few friends you can invite to join you. But most importantly, have fun before your study time begins.

Where do we find new members for our group?

Finding members can be challenging, especially for new groups that have only a few people or for existing groups that have lost a few people along the way. We encourage you to pray with your group and then brainstorm a list of people from work, church, your neighborhood, your children's school, family, the gym, and so forth. Use the five circles on page 178 to identify potential group members with whom you would like to build a spiritual friendship. Have each group member invite several people on his or her list.

No matter how you find members, it is vital that you stay on the lookout for new people to join your group. All groups tend to go through healthy attrition—the result of moves, sending out new leaders, ministry opportunities, and so forth—and if the group gets too small, it could be at risk of ending. If you and your group stay open to ideas, you will be amazed at the people God sends your way. The next person just might become a friend for life.

How long will this group meet?

Most groups meet weekly for at least their first six weeks, but every other week can work as well. We strongly recommend that the group meet for the first six months on a weekly basis if possible. This allows for continuity and, if people miss a meeting, they aren't gone for a whole month.

At the end of this study, group members may decide if they want to continue for another study. Some groups launch relationships for years to come, and others are steppingstones into another group experience. Either way, enjoy the journey.

Can we do this study on our own?

Absolutely! One of the best ways to do this study is not with a full house but with a few friends. You may choose to gather with another couple who would enjoy some relational time (perhaps going to the movies or having a quiet dinner) and then walking through this six-week study. Jesus will be with you even if there are only two of you (Matthew 18:20).

What if this group is not working for us?

Group changes are normal. They can be the result of a personality conflict, life stage difference, geographical distance, level of spiritual maturity, or any number of things. Relax. Pray for God's direction, and at the end of this six-week study, decide whether to continue with this group or find another. You don't typically buy the first car you test drive or marry the first person you date, and the same goes with a group. However, don't give up before the six weeks are up—God might have something to teach you. Also, don't run from conflict or judge people before you have given them a chance. God is still working in your life, too!

Who is the leader?

Most groups have an official leader. But ideally, the group will mature, and members will rotate the leadership of meetings. We have discovered that healthy groups rotate leaders and homes on a regular basis. This model ensures that all members grow, make their unique contributions, and develop their gifts. This study guide and the Holy Spirit can keep things on track even when you rotate leaders. Christ has promised to be in your midst as you gather. Ultimately, God is your leader each step of the way.

How do we handle the childcare needs in our group?

Child care can be a sensitive issue. We suggest that you empower the group to openly brainstorm solutions. You may try one option that works for a while and then adjust over time. Our favorite approach is for adults to meet in one room and share the cost of a babysitter (or two) who can watch the children in a different part of the house. This way, parents don't have to be away from their children all evening when their children are too young to be left at home. A second option is to use one home for the children and a second home (close by or a phone call away) for the adults. A third idea is to rotate the responsibility of providing a lesson or care for the children either in the same home or in another home nearby. This can be an incredible blessing for young families. Finally, the most common solution is to decide that you need to have a night to invest in your spiritual lives individually or as a couple and to make your own arrangements for childcare. No matter what decision the group makes, the best approach is to dialogue openly about both the need and the solution.

CIRCLES OF *life*

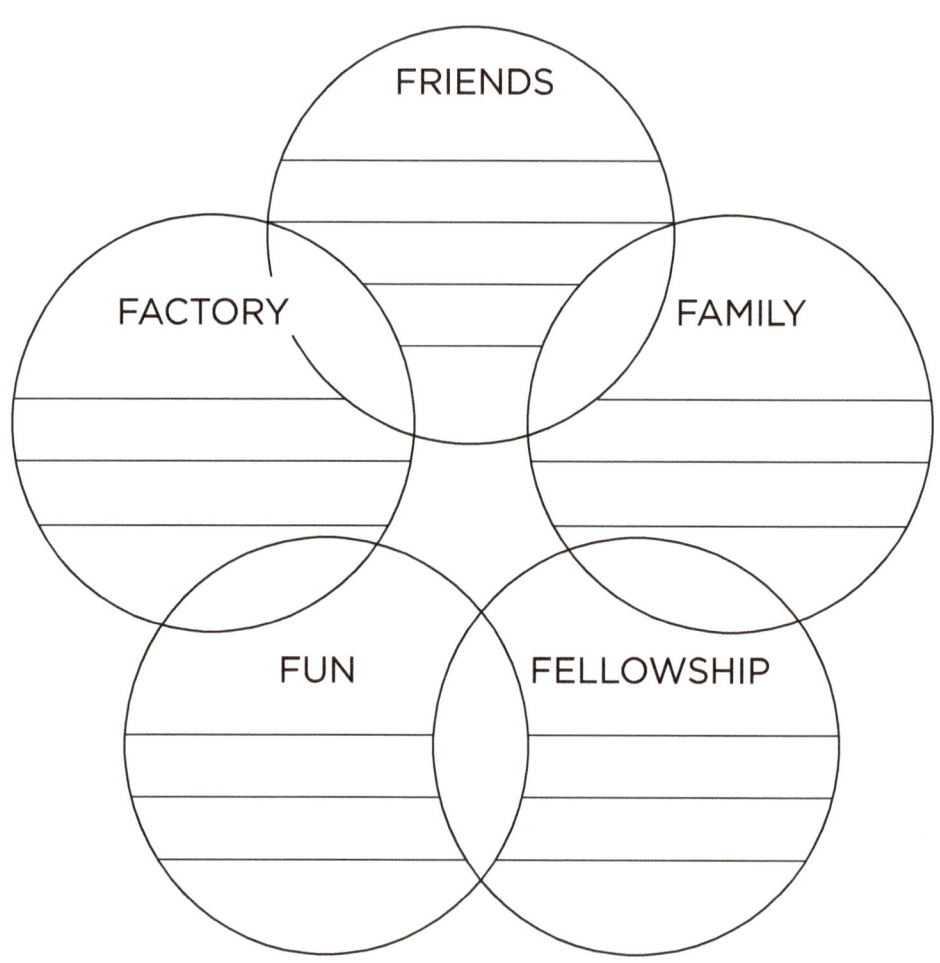

SMALL GROUP *covenant*

OUR PURPOSE
To provide a predictable environment where participants experience authentic Christian community to grow spiritually.

GROUP ATTENDANCE
To give priority to the group meeting. We will call or email if we will be late or absent. (Completing the Group Calendar on p. 180 will minimize this issue.)

SAFE ENVIRONMENT
To help create a safe place where people can be heard and feel loved. (Please, no quick answers, snap judgments, or simple fixes.)

RESPECT DIFFERENCES
To be gentle and gracious with different spiritual maturity levels, personal opinions, temperaments, or "imperfections" in fellow group members. We are all works in progress.

CONFIDENTIALITY
To keep anything that is shared strictly confidential and within the group, and to avoid sharing improper information about those outside the group.

ENCOURAGEMENT FOR GROWTH
To be not just takers, but givers of life. We want to spiritually multiply our lives by serving others with our God-given gifts.

SHARED OWNERSHIP
To remember that every member is a minister and to ensure that each attender will share a small team role or responsibility over time.

ROTATING HOSTS, FACILITATORS, AND HOMES
To encourage different people to host the group in their homes and to rotate the responsibility of facilitating each meeting. (See the Group Calendar on p. 180.)

SMALL GROUP *calendar*

Planning can help ensure the greatest participation at every meeting. At the end of each meeting, review this calendar. Be sure to include a regular rotation of host homes and facilitators, and don't forget birthdays, socials, church events, holidays, and ministry projects.

DATE	SESSION	HOST HOME

SNACKS	FACILITATOR

PRAYER & PRAISE *journal*

1

2

3

4

5

6

SMALL GROUP *roster*

NAME	EMAIL	CELL PHONE

SMALL GROUP *leader* HELP

HOSTING AN OPEN HOUSE

If you're starting a new group, try planning an Open House before your first formal group meeting. Even if you have only a few members, it's a great way to break the ice and prayerfully consider who else might be open to joining you over the next few weeks. You can also use this kick-off meeting to hand out books, spend some time getting to know each other, discuss each person's expectations for the group, and briefly pray for each other. A simple meal or dessert always make a kickoff meeting more fun. After people introduce themselves and share how they ended up being at the meeting (you can play a game to see who has the wildest story!), have everyone respond to a few icebreaker questions, such as:

- What is your favorite family vacation?
- What is one thing you love about your church?
- What is one thing about your life growing up that most people here don't know?

Next, ask everyone to tell what he or she hopes to get out of the study. You might want to review the Small Group Covenant on p. 149 and talk about each person's expectations and priorities. Finally, set an open chair (maybe two) in the center of your group and explain that it represents someone who would enjoy or benefit from this group who isn't here yet.

Ask people to pray about inviting someone to join the group over the next few weeks. Hand out postcards and have everyone write an invitation or two. Don't worry about ending up with too many people; you can always have one discussion circle in the living room and another in the dining room after you watch the lesson. Each group could then report prayer requests and progress at the end of the session.

You can skip this kickoff meeting if your time is limited, but you'll experience a huge benefit if you take the time to connect with one another in this way.

LEADING FOR THE *first* TIME

SEVEN COMMON LEADERSHIP EXPERIENCES.
WELCOME TO LIFE OUT IN FRONT!

Sweaty palms are a healthy sign. The Bible says that God is gracious to the humble. Remember who is in control; the time to worry is when you're not worried. God will work through those who are soft in heart (and sweaty-palmed).

Seek support. Ask your leader, co-leader, or a close friend to pray for you and prepare with you before the session. Walking through the study will help you anticipate potentially difficult questions and discussion topics.

Bring your uniqueness to the study. Lean into who you are and how God wants you to lead the study.

Prepare. Prepare. Prepare. Go through the session and read the section of Scripture. If you are using the video, listen to the teaching segment. Consider writing in a journal or praying through the day to prepare yourself for what God wants to do. Don't wait until the last minute to prepare.

Ask for feedback so you can grow. Perhaps in an email or on index cards handed out at the study, have everyone write down three things you did well and one thing you could improve on. Don't get defensive. Instead, show an openness to learn and grow.

Share with your group what God is doing in your heart. God is searching for those whose hearts are fully his. Share your trials and victories; people will relate.

Prayerfully consider whom you would like to pass the baton to next week. God is ready for the next member of your group to go on the faith journey you just traveled. Make it fun and expect God to do the rest.

LEADERSHIP *training* 101

Congratulations! You have responded to the call to help shepherd Jesus's flock. There are few other tasks in the family of God that surpass the contribution you will be making. As you prepare to lead, here are a few thoughts to keep in mind. We encourage you to read these and review them with each new discussion leader.

1. Remember that you are not alone. God knows everything about you, and he knew that you would be asked to lead this group. Remember that it is common for all good leaders to feel that they are not ready to lead. Moses, Solomon, Jeremiah, and Timothy were all reluctant to lead. God promises, *"I will never leave you nor forsake you"* (Hebrews 13:5). Whether you are leading for one evening, for several weeks, or for a lifetime, you will be blessed as you serve.

2. Don't try to do it alone. Pray right now for God to help you build a healthy leadership team. If you can enlist a co-leader to help you lead the group, you will find your experience to be much richer. This is your chance to involve as many people as you can in building a healthy group. All you have to do is call and ask people to help. You'll probably be surprised at the response.

3. Just be yourself. If you won't be you, who will? God wants you to use your unique gifts and temperament. Don't try to do things exactly like another leader; do them in a way that fits you! Just admit when you don't have an answer and apologize when you make a mistake. Your group will love you for it, and you'll sleep better at night!

4. Prepare for your meeting ahead of time. Review the session and write down your responses to each question. Pay special attention to exercises that ask group members to do something other than engage in discussion, like take an action. These exercises will help your group live what the Bible teaches, not just talk about it.

5. Pray for your group members by name. Before you begin your session, go around the room in your mind and pray for each member. Ask God to use your time together to touch the heart of every person uniquely. Expect God to lead you to whomever he wants you to encourage or challenge in a special way. If you listen, God will surely lead!

6. When you ask a question, be patient. Someone will eventually respond. Sometimes people need a moment or two of silence to think about the question. Keep in mind, if silence doesn't bother you, it won't bother anyone else. After someone responds, affirm the response with a simple "thanks" or "good job." Then ask, "How about somebody else?" or "Would someone who hasn't shared like to add anything?" Be sensitive to new people or members who aren't ready to share. If you give them a safe setting, they will blossom over time.

7. Provide transitions between questions. When guiding the discussion, always read aloud the transitional paragraphs and the questions. Ask the group if anyone would like to read the paragraphs or Bible passages. Don't call on anyone, but ask for volunteers; then be patient until someone begins. Be sure to thank the people who read aloud.

8. Break up into small groups each week or a larger group won't stay. If your group has a lot of people, we strongly encourage you to have the group gather sometimes in discussion circles of three or four people during the **Encounter the Word, Engage Our Hearts, and Encourage Others** sections of the study. With a greater opportunity to talk in small circles, people will connect more with the study, apply more quickly what they're learning, and ultimately get more out of it. A small circle also encourages a quiet person to participate and minimizes the effect of a more dominant or vocal member. It can also help people feel more loved in your group.

    When you gather again at the end of the section, you can have one person summarize the highlights from each circle. Small circles are also helpful during prayer time. People who are not accustomed to praying aloud will feel more comfortable trying it with just two or three others.

    Also, prayer requests won't take as much time, so circles will have more time to actually pray. When you gather back with the whole group, you can have one person from each circle briefly update everyone on the prayer requests. People are more willing to break into small circles to pray if they know the whole group will hear all the prayer requests.

9. Rotate facilitators weekly. At the end of each meeting, ask the group who should lead the following week. Let the group help select your weekly facilitator. You may be perfectly capable of leading each time, but you will help others grow in their faith and gifts if you give them opportunities to lead. You can use the Small Group Calendar (p. 180) to fill in the names of the different leaders for all the meetings if you prefer.

10. One final challenge (for new or first-time leaders): Before your first opportunity to lead, look up each of the five passages listed below. Read each one as a devotional exercise to help equip yourself with a shepherd's heart. Trust us on this one. If you do this, you will be more than ready to lead your first meeting.

www.ingramcontent.com/pod-product-compliance
Lightning Source LLC
Chambersburg PA
CBHW042112120526
44592CB00042B/2713